PEOPLE IN ORGANIZATIONS

WHAT EVERY MANAGER SHOULD KNOW ABOUT HUMAN RESOURCES

Donald E. O'Neal, Ph.D

Professor of Management
University of Illinois Springfield

american press

BOSTON, MASSACHUSETTS
www.americanpresspublishers.com

ACKNOWLEDGEMENTS

This book was developed to provide students, particularly non-traditional students who continue working while they complete their education, with a textbook that concentrates on fundamentals that every manager, in every organization, should know about working with people (i.e., managing human resources.) I feel it meets that goal, but the final judges will be those who use it: students, practicing managers and leaders, and business owners.

I must acknowledge my students, past, present, and future. They are the inspiration for what I do; they help me understand how they learn; they provide invaluable feedback on what works and what doesn't, even long after they've graduated; and they continue teaching me how to teach them.

I owe a lasting debt of gratitude to the professors who have taught and guided me and continue to do so, and the colleagues with whom I have had the good fortune to work and study.

The support and understanding of my wife, Nancy, has been essential to developing this project from a rough idea.

The helpful guidance of my editor, Marci Taylor, has been invaluable in converting my thoughts, ideas, and writing into a published product.

Finally, reading the book or scanning the References section should give the reader some idea of the number of other writers who have influenced my thinking. This book is an integration of thoughts and ideas selected from many sources, as well as from my own experience in the classroom, in corporate management, and consulting with a variety of organizations. I am grateful to all whose thoughts and ideas have influenced my thinking.

No matter how conscientious I may have been, this book is, and will continue to be, a work in progress, and I welcome any suggestions for correction or improvement, or for additional topics or examples.

Don O'Neal
Professor of Management
University of Illinois Springfield
oneal.don@uis.edu

PREFACE

My first formal experience in human resources began when my CEO asked me to develop a Human Resource Department for our company.

The company had grown very quickly during the previous five years, to the point where a personnel department that had been created to meet the hiring and record-keeping requirements of a start-up company was now struggling to service the needs of an organization with more than 500 employees.

Although I had been a manager for a number of years, the CEO's request caught me completely by surprise, since I was an engineering manager, with no experience in human resources. Nor had I had any education or training in the field. But when I brought that to his attention, he assured me that he had considered those issues before offering me the assignment.

When I asked "Why me?" the CEO replied that he had considered two possibilities: hire an experienced human resource professional from outside the company, or promote someone from inside the company; someone, he emphasized, the employees trusted.

One of his concerns was that the company had recently emerged from a failed attempt to unionize its workforce—an attempt organized by a group of workers who didn't trust their supervisors. As a result, the CEO considered trust a major factor in whether or not the new department and its leader would succeed or fail. After considering both courses of action, he concluded that the company would be better off going with someone who was already trusted than with an outsider who would have to *earn* their trust. Realizing that earning trust is a slow process, he was concerned that there might not be enough time before another unionizing attempt.

So I became Director of Human Resources, an area about which I knew almost nothing, at least not from a human resource perspective. However, as it turned out, my management experience in other areas served me better than any amount of education or training in human resources might have.

When I had been made a manager for the first time, several years before, it was through the same process experienced by most new managers during those days. One day, without prior notice, I was informed that I was being promoted to a supervisory position, starting the next day. And I learned that I would be managing those who had been my co-workers: people who were my colleagues and friends.

So my first experience in management was under the most difficult of circumstances: managing people who had been my close associates; which is immeasurably more difficult than managing strangers. In addition, I was faced with learning how to manage by trial and error, rather than through education, training, and experience. The point I'm making is that managing or supervising people, and doing it well, is not an easy assignment, and certainly not one that should be learned entirely on the job.

That's why one of the purposes of this book is to serve as a how-to handbook for people who aspire to supervise other people. It was written to help them learn how to deal with the many different situations, dilemmas, and problems they will ultimately face in working with people.

Let's go back, for a minute, to when I first became Director of Human Resources. One advantage of the trial-and-error method of learning to manage is that it gave me an entirely different perspective on people and their problems than I could have learned from a book or in the classroom. I soon learned that there are *no right answers*, and just how many wrong answers there are. Every situation is different, because all people are different.

So my lack of education and training in human resource management turned out to be much more of a blessing than a curse.

It was curse in the sense that I knew much less about the subject than the human resource people I was now supervising, and that I didn't have a clear concept of where to begin. On the positive side, my management experience had given me an entirely different perspective than that of someone experienced in human resource management. I came in without any preconceived notions of how such a department should operate, so I wasn't hampered by tradition. And, since the company had very few human resource processes in place, I could build new ones from scratch.

That gave me an opportunity to research how other companies were addressing the challenges of human resource management, and to learn what were best-practices in the field. In the process, I learned about state-of-the-art human resource practices in areas such as compensation, recruiting, performance management, benefits, and incentives.

That allowed me, as I designed and developed our processes and programs, to benchmark them against the best in the field, rather than just copying what was traditional, or standard practice in the industry. The result was a philosophy of human resources that was based on best practices, common sense and, most important, practical application.

Some years later, when I began teaching human resources at a major university, I started out using traditional textbooks. But it didn't take long to see that the students were much more interested in the practical application—the "how-to"—of human resource policies and procedures, than they were in the theories behind them.

So I gradually began moving away from standard textbooks, increasingly relying on my own notes and personal examples. And it wasn't long before I began to see major improvements in students' interest, learning, and retention.

They began coming to class with their own anecdotes about how they had applied class concepts in their organizations, and how effective those concepts were. To me, the ultimate judgment of how much people have learned is how effectively they can apply what they've learned. And the best gauge of the value of the subject matter is how well it works in practice.

This book, then, is a synthesis of my own management experience, my class notes and personal anecdotes that illustrate the concepts. It's important to note the difference between this book and other human resource textbooks. Whereas most books on the subject are written more for human resource professionals, this one is written for managers and supervisors in all areas, and at all levels in an organization. It was developed as more of a handbook than a textbook—a practical guide to managing people in organizations

It is based on two basic philosophies: 1) that people in organizations should be *developed*, not managed; and 2) that human resource management should be the primary responsibility of every supervisor, manager, and leader in the organization; *not* just the human resource department.

Perhaps the major benefit of my management experience has been the values and beliefs that I developed, which have become the foundation of this book. The philosophy that guides my perspective on how to work with people, and how to lead them, is based on one primary concept: *trust*—mutual trust between managers and the people who are their responsibility.

Without trust, managers can only try to *control* workers; *with* trust, they can *empower* people. Without trust, people are just tools—"human resources"—to be used by managers. With trust, *people are the organization*, and the keys to their managers' success, not to mention the success of the organization.

Laws are written to protect people against injustice. Toward that end, virtually every labor law that exists was written to prevent organizations and their managers from mistreating their workers, because many organizations had mistreated their workers. As a result, organizations today worry about the thousands of labor laws that can affect them. But, ironically, all a company and its managers would have to do to avoid breaking those laws is to treat people fairly; treat them right; treat them the way *you* would like to be treated.

With that in mind, this book doesn't devote much space to the legal aspects of human resource management. The basic things that are most important to people aren't much different today than they were thousands of years ago, and they aren't likely to be much different in the future. The laws are sure to change, but the things that are most important to people will remain as they always have: safety, security, fair treatment, self-esteem, recognition, appreciation, friends and family. Helping provide and protect their employees' rights to those should be a primary consideration of every organization, and of every supervisor, manager, and executive, at every level of the organization. The organization whose managers focus on treating people right has little to fear from labor laws.

A final note:

Although I have used the term "human resources" throughout this preface, it's a term I don't particularly like. To me it portrays people as indistinguishable pieces of raw material, stacked somewhere in a storage area awaiting a situation into which they can be inserted. "Human resources" is an archaic term; a throwback to the time when organizations primarily hired uneducated, unskilled workers, and treated them like interchangeable automons, who were fit only to follow orders.

Nothing could be further from today's reality, in which people, and the knowledge that they bring with them, are the keys to every organization's success. These are not "human resources," nor are they "employees;" they are *people,* whose individuality and value to their companies should be recognized and honored.

CONTENTS

Preface ....

Introduction ....

PART I—INTRODUCTION
       TO HUMAN RESOURCE MANAGEMENT 1

---

1 The Role of Human Resource Management 3
   Organizations 3
   People.. 3
   Purpose.. 4
       The Internal Environment 5
       The External Environment 6
       Policies and Procedures 7
   Benefits 7
   Summary 8

2 Organizational Strategy
   and Human Resource Management 9
   Summary 13

3 History of Human Resource Management 15
   HR 1—Helping Workers Adjust 16
   HR 2—Labor Relations.................................. 17
   HR 3—Risk Aversion..................................... 17
   HR 4—Strategic HRM 17
   Summary 18

xi

4 Human Resource Theories 19
Type I—Universal Principles 19
Type 2—The social Nature of Organizations 22
Type 3—The Contingency Approach 24
Type 4—The Political Nature of Organizations 26
Summary 27

PART II—STAFFING **31**

---

5 Planning **33**
Strategic Planning 33
Job Design 34
   Job Descriptions 34
   Job Responsibilities 35
Staffing Levels 36
Summary 37

6 Recruiting **39**
Internal Recruiting 40
   Locating Candidates 41
External Recruiting 43
   Recruiting Area 44
   Sources of Candidates 44
Summary 49

7 Selection **51**
Information 51
   Screening 52
   Background Checks 52
Testing 54
Interviewing 55
   Qualifications 55

Personality 55
Interviewers 56
Selection Decision 57
Qualifications 58
Attitude 59
Summary 61

PART III—DEVELOPING PEOPLE 65

8 Orientation 67
Purpose 69
Presentation 70
Content 70
Benefits 71
Summary 72

9 Training 73
Needs 73
Types of Training 74
Non-Managerial 75
Managerial/Supervisory 76
Special Training 77
Learning 77
Trainers 78
Summary 79

10 Career Development 81
Responsibility 81
The Individual 83
The Organization 84
Summary 86

11 Performance 87

Goals 87

Evaluating Performance 89

Improving Performance 91

    Abilities 91

    Behavior 92

Performance Evaluation Programs 94

Summary 95

PART IV—REWARDING PERFORMANCE 97

12 Compensation 99

Compensation Programs 99

    Objectives 100

    Policies 100

Wage Components 100

    Internal Factors 100

    External Factors 101

Job Evaluation 101

    Job Ranking 101

    Job Classification 103

    The Point System 104

    Factor Comparison 104

Wages 106

Performance 108

    Pay for Performance 108

    Skill-Based Pay 110

Compensation Issues 111

Government Regulation 112

Summary 113

13 Incentives 115
Motivation 115
Incentives 116
Rewards 117
Needs 118
Incentive Programs 121
    Requirements for Success 121
    Barriers to Success 122
    Management/Professional Incentives 123
    Sales Incentives 125
    Executive Incentives 126
    Productivity Incentives 127
Non-Monetary Incentives 131
Summary 133

14 Benefits 137
Benefit Programs 137
    Flexible Benefit Plans 138
    Communication 138
Mandatory Benefits 139
    Social Security Insurance 139
    Workers' Compensation Insurance 140
    Unemployment Insurance 140
    Unpaid Leaves 140
Discretionary Benefits 141
    Healthcare Insurance 141
    Life Insurance 141
    Payment for Time Not Worked 142
    Pension Plans 143
    Employee Services 145
    Other Services 147
    Summary 147

PART V—LEADERSHIP	....	**149**

15 **Leadership and Management** **151**
Leadership vs. Management 151
Self-Awareness 155
    Attitude 155
    Capabilities 156
    Personal Responsibility 158
Courage 159
    Commitment 159
    Sacrifice 160
    Unselfishness 161
Delegation/Empowerment 162
    Empowerment 163
    Delegation 164
Strategic Thinking 164
Summary 166

16 **Communication** **169**
Sending 169
Receiving 173
Understanding 173
Questions 176
Upward Communication 178
Summary 180

17 **The Organization's Atmosphere** **183**
Culture 185
Social Responsibility 187
Values 188
Employee Satisfaction 190
Summary 192

18 **The External Environment** **195**
Opportunities and Threats 197
Managing the External Environment 198
Summary 204

19 **Moving into the Future** **205**
Change 205
Leading Change 207
Downsizing 211
Future Challenges/Opportunities 213
Summary 216

References **217**

INTRODUCTION

*"Always human beings will live and progress
to greater, broader, and fuller life."*
(William E.B. Du Bois, 1868-1963)

From the beginning of the Industrial Revolution, which began in the middle 1800s and continued until the late 1900s, the majority of organizations viewed their people as a homogeneous group of anonymous, faceless, interchangeable resources. Managers believed that one person was about the same as any other, and all were easily replaceable.

While that may still be the perspective in some parts of the world, particularly in less-developed countries, in the United States this view changed significantly as organizations became increasingly knowledge-based.

By knowledge-based, I mean the value of an organization's products or services comes from what the organization knows, or knows how to do, that other organizations don't know; the organization's competitive success comes from its knowledge.

While knowledge is important to every organization, the difference between a knowledge-based organization and one that is product- or service-based, is the *source* of its knowledge—where the knowledge comes from; where it's located.

When organizations hired mostly unskilled workers, they developed methods and procedures to closely guide what those workers did and how they did it. In that setting, workers weren't hired for their knowledge, but for their physical capabilities and energy. Organizations only wanted workers' bodies, not their minds; in fact, they preferred that their workers not think at all. One of the primary roles of supervisors and managers was to tell workers exactly what to do and how to do it. Most jobs were broken into a series of small tasks, so that each worker had to do only one or two simple operations—tighten one or two bolts on each product, for example—hour after hour, day after day, and month after month. Tasks were so simple workers could learn them quickly, and could almost do them in their sleep.

Under those conditions, any worker who left an organization could be easily and quickly replaced. The knowledge of how to do their job remained in the organization, in the form of documents describing the methodology—how each job was to be done. So the organization's knowledge was retained by the organization.

But today's economy is dominated by knowledge-based organizations; organizations made up of knowledge workers: educated people, professionals, and specialists who are hired for what they know and what they know how to do. The major difference between knowledge-based organizations and those that base their operations primarily on unskilled workers is the *source* of the organization's knowledge.

In a traditional organization, the knowledge is developed within the organization, and remains there in the form of its documented methods and procedures. As workers leave the company, the knowledge stays.

But knowledge-based organizations *hire* their knowledge; it comes into the company in the minds of its people, and when they leave their knowledge goes with them. That makes employee turnover a major concern. Retaining people whose knowledge is unique is much more essential than retaining non-skilled people, who can easily be replaced.

That gets to one of the primary premises of this book: how to find the people with the knowledge and capabilities the organization needs, then *select, develop* and *retain* them.

Another premise is that selecting, developing, and retaining people, should *not* be the sole responsibility of an organization's Human Resource Department; it should also be a primary responsibility of every supervisor and manager in the organization. The most important responsibilities of any Human Resource Department should be developing, implementing, and overseeing the organization's human resource policies, programs, and procedures, and maintaining personnel records. Beyond that it should be available to managers and supervisors as a resource: a provider of the expertise, services, and information they need.

In that role, the HR department should *assist* the organization's managers in:

- finding, analyzing, and selecting suitable candidates,
- developing people,
- evaluating and improving peoples' performance,
- determining proper compensation,
- providing appropriate disciplinary actions.

Repeating: the human resource department should assist managers, as requested, but *not* do these things *for* them.

In short, every manager in the organization should be a human resource manager, not just those in the Human Resource department. With that in mind, this book is written to help managers and supervisors learn and apply the principles of effectively working with, developing, and leading people in organizations.

The book is organized into five sections:

Part I is an Introduction to Human Resource Management; what it is, what it does, and why it is important (Chapter 1, The

Role of Human Resource Management); how it relates to an organization's strategy (Chapter 2, Organizational Strategy and Human Resource Management); the history of human resource management, and how it has evolved (Chapter 3, History of Human Resource Management); and the theories that have driven its evolution (Chapter 4, Human Resource Theories.)

Part II describes what I consider the primary function of HRM: Staffing; how to assess what kinds of people and abilities the organization needs (Chapter 5, Planning); how and where to find qualified candidates (Chapter 6, Recruiting); and how to select the people who will best meet the organization's needs (Chapter 7, Selection.)

Part III focuses on what I feel is the most neglected role of HRM, Developing people. Chapter 8, Orientation, discusses the importance of properly introducing new people to the organization and its purpose, values, philosophies, and history. Chapter 9, Training, describes the role of training, and when and how it should be done. Chapter 10, Career Development, emphasizes the importance of helping people within the organization plan and develop their careers. And Chapter 11, Performance, shows how to help each person improve his/her performance through effective evaluation and measurement.

Part IV, Rewarding Performance, is a natural follow-up to performance evaluation: how to reward people for their performance. Chapter 12 addresses Compensation; Chapter 13, Incentives, and Chapter 14, Benefits.

Whereas Part I introduces HRM, and Parts II—IV focus on the organization's most important resource, people, Part V is designed to show managers the difference between traditional theories and methods of management, and why they are now largely out of date and counterproductive.

Chapter 15, Leadership and Management, describes the differences between Leadership and Management, when and where each is most appropriate, and why today's managers need to be more leaders than managers. Chapter 16, Communication, discusses the importance of effective communication among people at all levels, especially between managers and their workers. Chapter 17, The Organization's Atmosphere, demonstrates the importance of organizational culture and values, and how they affect employee satisfaction. Chapter 18, The External Environment, discusses the importance of managers, at all levels, knowing what's going on in the world outside the organization, and how that information can affect the organization's success. Finally, Chapter 19, Moving into the Future, describes the necessity of having a forward-looking perspective.

Overall, the major premise of this book is that, in the future, the managers who will be most effective will be those who focus most of their attention on providing the forward-looking direction that will lead their people and the organization to future success, then selecting and developing the people who will make that future happen. And the book's primary purpose is to help every manager and supervisor become that kind of leader.

PART I

INTRODUCTION TO HUMAN RESOURCE MANAGEMENT

Much has been written about human resource management, most of it is from the perspective of managing a human resource *department,* usually with a strong emphasis on legal concerns. This book focuses on what every manager (not just those in human resources) should understand about people, not as human resources, but as *individuals.*

The chapters in this section discuss the role of human resource management, how it relates to the organization's strategic plan, the history of human resource management and how it has evolved, and the theories and assumptions that have driven that evolution.

1 | THE ROLE OF HUMAN RESOURCE MANAGEMENT

"To protect the workers
in their inalienable rights to a higher and better life;..."
(Samuel Gompers, 1850-1924)

ORGANIZATIONS

Our lives revolve around organizations, like schools, churches, sports teams, social clubs and, of course, the organizations where we work. Every one of these organizations was initially created for a specific purpose: to achieve something; to accomplish some goal. Just what are those purposes, and why do people join organizations?

PEOPLE

For the most part, we all join organizations because they help us accomplish things that we can't get done by ourselves. So we could say a primary purpose of any organization is to help people help each other. But, at the same time, people *are* the organization; without people there would be no organizations, nor any need for them.

You may have noticed my use of the term "people," rather than "human resources." As I've said before, that's because I don't particularly like "human resources. To me it's an inventory term, implying that people are just another form of raw material.

Perhaps that came about during the early years of the industrial revolution, when jobs were so simple almost anyone could do them, and workers could easily be replaced, just like the interchangeable parts of a machine. From that perspective maybe workers *were* just "human resources," but that's not true any more.

In recent years productivity improvements have dramatically reduced the need for unskilled workers, while increasing the demand for "knowledge workers": people whose education and training make them invaluable to their companies because of the knowledge they bring with them.

Knowledge workers are not interchangeable; each is valuable for his/her unique knowledge, skills, and abilities, so they are no longer "human resources," they are people; individuals who will not respond well to being treated like "resources."

That said, throughout this book you'll find frequent references to human resources," because that term has become ingrained in the language of the "people" industry. But I've tried to limit it to use as an adjective, in describing *things* (e.g., "human resource program," "human resource management"), and to avoid using it as a noun, referring to people.

PURPOSE

The purpose of human resource management (HRM) is to help an organization hire and retain the people it needs to accomplish its purpose (mission.) But what does "help the organization" mean? And *who* in the organization is HRM expected to help?

The answer to both questions is "to help top management" help them find the people he organization needs. But that's not all; once those people have been hired, the organization has a responsibility to help *them*, a responsibility that normally falls to the human resource department. Help new employees in what way?

An old adage has it that a human resource department has two responsibilities: to protect the people from the company, and to protect the company from its people. Of course, that's just another way of saying "balancing the needs of the company with the needs of its employees," but even that doesn't go quite far enough.

A human resource department should also serve as the conscience of the company, a responsibility that involves balancing the way the company responds to the needs of *all* of its stakeholders. That includes not just management and employees, but also the owners/stockholders, customers, local community, government, and the environment.

Balancing stakeholder needs means ensuring fair and equitable treatment of employees, fair return on investment for the owners, fair value for customers, and being socially responsible as a corporate citizen of the community and the world.

However, no matter how hard the organization works to balance those needs, it will never be able to completely satisfy all stakeholders, because of the realities and limitations imposed by its internal and external environments.

The Internal Environment

An organization's internal environment affects its capabilities in physical, technological, social, political and economic ways.

Physical

The physical environment of the workplace, including factors like safety, noise levels, temperature, and air quality, can influence employees' ability and willingness to do the work, and may require higher wages for some types of jobs.

Technological

Work processes, equipment, and the layout of the workplace can affect how jobs are done, interaction among employees, cooperation and conflict, and formal and informal work groups.

Social

The organization's culture will affect the attitudes and behavior of employees as well as their managers.

Political

Those with the most power in the organization, be it official power or informal power, will have the greatest influence on the organization's agendas, and on what gets done, and how.

Economic

The organization's financial condition is likely to limit what it is *able* to do, while the moves of its competitors will influence what it *actually* does, and *how*.

The External Environment

Like its internal environment, an organization's external environment can limit its capabilities in physical, technological, social, political and economic ways.

Physical

Where the organization is located, including the area's climate and the strength of the local economy, can affect its ability to attract and retain workers, and how much it will have to pay them.

Technological

Its technology will affect the number of workers required, what skills and knowledge will be needed, the kinds of training required, and the rate of change within the organization.

Social

Changing social norms make freedom of choice and individual rights more important to workers, particularly as they become more concerned with balancing their work and personal lives

Political

Constantly changing local, state, and federal laws create an ongoing challenge for organizations.

Economic

A constant concern is the supply of, and demand for, knowledge workers. The more competition there is for their services, the more wages, benefits, and company loyalty are affected.

Policies and Procedures

Its human resource programs are the way an organization responds to its internal and external environments. The behavior, actions, and decisions of the organization's managers are guided by policies and procedures that are designed to cover the situations they are most likely to encounter.

BENEFITS

An effective human resource management program will have at least two major benefits:

• helping the organization achieve its goals,
• helping people achieve their personal goals.

In addition, it will help managers, at all levels, become more effective, which will result in increased employee satisfaction, higher productivity, decreased employee turnover, and a more successful organization.

SUMMARY

The role of human resource management is to help the organization hire the people it needs, and to ensure that they remain with the organization.

As simple as that may sound, it is a complicated process, involving balancing the needs of the company with the personal needs of its employees.

The result will be high levels of employee satisfaction, high productivity, low employee turnover, and greater organizational success.

But it's important to remember that those results cannot be accomplished by the human resource department, alone. It will take the collective and cooperative efforts of everyone in the organization. The primary role of the human resource department is not managing the organization's human resources; it is providing the programs, policies, and procedures that will enable every manager, at every level, to be an effective human resource manager, and an effective leader of his/her people.

2 | ORGANIZATIONAL STRATEGY AND HUMAN RESOURCE MANAGEMENT

"...all power is a trust; ...
we are accountable for its exercise; ..."
(Benjamin Disraeli, 1804-1881)

An organization's strategic plan is its map of the future. It defines the organization's mission: its purpose, why it exists, what business its in.

As I've previously emphasized, the key to an organization's future is its people, so they are essential to its strategy. It's people who develop the strategic plan, including the organization's mission, goals, and the strategies and action plans that will ensure the goals are achieved and the mission accomplished.

But that's just the beginning. A strategic plan is only the first of a two-part process. Once the plan has been developed, it must be implemented; put into action. And who will implement it? People; they will take the actions that will make the plan come to life. So people are the key to the success of a strategic plan, at both levels: planning and implementation.

But not just *any* people; different strategies often require different people. The success of any strategic plan depends on an organization having a distinctive competence: some unique set of capabilities, knowledge, resources, and/or technology that will make its products or services more attractive to customers than those of the competition.

Because that uniqueness is so often based on the specialized knowledge, skills and abilities of its people, whenever an organi-

9

zation changes its competitive strategy, it is likely to need new knowledge, skills, and abilities. And those can only be acquired either through the training and education of existing employees, or by hiring new people. Obviously, either approach will require the assistance of the organization's human resource programs. Let's look at an example:

Suppose you work for an electric utility company, one that has operated under government regulation for its entire history. But you've recently learned that the government will de-regulate your industry, two years from now.

In a regulated environment your company has been a monopoly, providing electricity for a defined group of customers for whom there are no other providers; no other companies that offer the same services.

But in the future, operating in a de-regulated market, you'll have to compete for customers; compete with other companies who will be trying to attract the same customers. In fact they'll be trying to attract the customers who have always been exclusively *yours*. With that scenario in mind, let's compare your company as it is now, with how it will need to be, to compete successfully in the future.

Right now, operating in a protected environment, you're insulated from the outside world; insulated in the sense that you don't have to worry about a major uncertainty: competition. Have you ever thought about the advantages of a protected monopolist? What it's like to "compete" when there is no competition?

With no competition you don't have to be concerned with market share. You have it *all*, and with your market share guaranteed, you don't need a distinctive competence, because your customers have no choice: they either buy from your company or do without. And you don't have to worry about other companies entering our industry; they're prohibited by law.

Without competition, your company has been able to operate pretty much the same way year after year. You haven't had to worry about controlling costs, or providing better products or services, or superior customer service. And, perhaps most important, you haven't had to worry about profits. The law has allowed you to set prices at whatever level enables you to maintain a reasonable profit, over and above your operating costs. And whenever your operating costs have gone up, you've been allowed to increase your prices accordingly.

So you've had little incentive to improve your products, services, or processes. As a result, your organizational culture has become complacent, set in its ways ("if it ain't broke, don't fix it"), and not very innovative. Furthermore, you've had no compelling reason to be concerned about what other companies in your industry are doing.

That's been organizational life in the cozy cocoon of a non-competitive industry. But how successful would that same company be in *competitive* environment? Probably not competitive at all, at least without some major changes.

First, you'd need an entirely different organizational strategy; a *competitive* strategy; based on some type of distinctive competence. You might differentiate your company by offering higher quality, better reliability, or superior customer service; something that will make customers prefer you over your competitors. Or you could simply price your products and services lower than the competition.

Whichever strategy you choose will require some combination of increased innovation, lower costs, better customer service, better equipment, and/or a greater concern for public relations. In short, you would need a more dynamic culture; one that complements your competitive strategies.

What would this kind of change in corporate strategy mean, from a human resource perspective?

First, you'd have to change the organizational culture, from passive and complacent to dynamic and competitive. That would involve major education and training for most, if not all, existing employees, requiring considerable time, and lost productivity.

Unfortunately, there would undoubtedly be some people who couldn't adapt to such a dramatic shift in required behavior, which might lead to layoffs, perhaps involving a significant number of workers.

The need for new knowledge, skills, and abilities, in areas such as sales, marketing, and innovation, would mean recruiting new people. The organization's incentive and reward system may have to change significantly, to support the need for higher productivity and greater efficiency.

And the organization's structure is almost certain to change, from bureaucratic and mechanistic to more organic and flexible; to a structure better positioned to respond effectively to a changing competitive environment.

And, of course, an essential part of that overall transformation will be developing the ability to manage change, both within the organization and in its external environment.

At this point, it's important to notice that in this example we've only discussed the changes that will be necessary in an organization moving from a monopoly to a competitive environment. We haven't even touched on the HR challenges associated with global strategies, mergers and acquisitions, or significant organizational growth.

So you can see that organizational strategy can have, and ultimately *will* have, a major impact on human resource programs, policies, and procedures, as well as on the human resources, themselves.

SUMMARY

Human resource management plays a key role in organizational strategy. As we've previously emphasized, organizations *are* people: people develop the strategies and people implement them.

But while emphasizing the importance of people, we mustn't lose sight of the essential relationship between organizational strategy and human resource management: the strategy should always come *first*. Strategy should determine the human resource activities, *not* the reverse. As important as the human resource program is, it exists to *serve* the organization, not to *lead* it.

With that in mind, an organization's human resource programs and activities are so essential they can either make or break a strategy. The unqualified support of the human resource program can ensure the organization's success, or its resistance can become an insurmountable obstacle.

3	# THE HISTORY OF HUMAN RESOURCE MANAGEMENT

*"People are difficult to govern
because they have too much knowledge."*

(Lao-tzu, 604-531 B.C.)

The economy of the United States was dominated by agriculture until the mid-1800s, when industrialization quickly began to increase in importance. A major driver of the industrial revolution was the steam engine, which had been developed in England, and represented the first *moveable* source of power.

Before the steam engine, organizations had to depend on either wind or water as sources of power. That, of course, meant they had to locate near rivers, or in areas with dependable prevailing winds. The steam engine freed companies from those constraints, and allowed them to locate anywhere they chose.

Steam power wasn't just portable, it had another major advantage: it was virtually unlimited. The amount of power was no longer limited by the size of a river or the strength of the wind. Companies could now have as much power as they needed, which gave them the opportunity to grow; to become as large as they wanted to be. And, since increased size allowed for economies of scale, organizations quickly began getting bigger.

Larger organizations led to an increased demand for workers, most of whom initially came from farms; attracted by the prospect of more money and easier lives. But the supply of farm folk was soon outstripped by the rapidly-increasing demand for workers, so employers began searching for other sources.

The demand was finally satisfied by opening U.S. borders to immigration, and encouraging workers from other countries to settle here. But immigration brought new problems for employers, foremost among them language barriers. Although the immigrants were able and willing to work, most of them didn't speak English, nor did they understand it. And, of course, their supervisors were in similar straights: most of them only understood one language: English. Thus developed the first need for human resource management: helping immigrant workers adjust.

HR 1—HELPING WORKERS ADJUST

The first venture of most organizations into human resource management was hiring people to teach immigrants English, and to help them adjust to the working environment, and to their new country. Some companies even took a paternalistic approach to helping immigrants, trying to treat them like "family," and setting them up in "company towns."

Those first human resource programs included industrial psychologists to help select workers, social welfare people to help them adjust, and teachers to help them learn English, and throughout the process leadership and common sense prevailed.

But not all companies treated their employees fairly; some treated them like "resources," using them at will, sometimes abusing them in the process, and discarding them when they were worn out, or when the company no longer needed them. To defend themselves against these injustices, workers began joining together, to attempt to bargain collectively with their companies.

The original purpose of this unionization was to demand fair treatment and better and safer working conditions. But these attempts at collective bargaining were quickly rebuffed by management, resulting in negotiations that were more adversarial than cooperative.

HR 2—LABOR RELATIONS

In response to their employees forming unions, organizations changed the role of human resource management, from helping workers to managing relations with labor unions. This included mediating between management and employee unions, negotiating with union representatives, and arbitrating grievances. The role of human resource management shifted from a cooperative relationship with people to an adversarial relationship with their unions.

And this remained the dominant role of human resource management until the Civil Rights Act of 1964 was signed into law.

HR 3—RISK AVERSION

Under the Civil Rights Act, some companies, particularly those whose human resource practices were questionable, became concerned with the possibility of lawsuits, and their approach to human resource management shifted primarily to risk aversion: trying to reduce the risk of lawsuits.

HR 4—STRATEGIC HRM

Risk aversion remained a primary concern of human resource management until the 1980s, by which time most organizations had begun to realize that human resources were a strategic necessity; a key to the organization's competitive success.

This change in perception was brought about by a number of forces, including:

- the increasing importance of knowledge workers,
- changing societal values,
- increasing government regulation,
- technological change,
- increased concern for productivity,
- globalization,
- demographic changes.

Fortunately the success of this approach to human resource management has increasingly influenced organizations to recognize how dependent they are on their people, and to adopt human resource policies that reflect that concern.

SUMMARY

Throughout its history, the role of human resource management has changed, from helping people, to resisting unions, to avoiding lawsuits, and now it seems to have come full circle: back to helping people.

Whereas the methodology is somewhat different, the intent is once again based on the knowledge that organizations need people, and the role of human resource management should be, first, to help find those people and, second, to help keep them.

4 | HUMAN RESOURCE THEORIES

"Man, unlike any other thing ... in the universe,
grows beyond his work, ..."
(John Steinbeck, 1902-1968)

Human resource practices have been heavily influenced by organization theory which, Robbins suggests, can be traced back to biblical times "...one of the most enduring and successful models ...[of organization design is] the simple hierarchy of the Roman Catholic Church. Its five-level design has proven effective for nearly 2000 years." (1990:33)

There have been countless other examples through the years, but the theories that have had the biggest effect on human resource practices began in the early 1900s, led by four major schools of thought about how organizations view their people. Robbins (1990) classifies them as Types 1, 2, 3, and 4 theorists.

TYPE 1—UNIVERSAL PRINCIPLES (1900-1930)

This perspective focused on developing guidelines for how to manage people—guidelines that would work in *any* organization—and was dominated by three theorists:

Frederick Taylor—Scientific Management

His *Principles of Scientific Management*, which were based on his own scientific research, focused on four principles that Taylor was convinced would significantly increase productivity:

1. Scientific determination of how to do each job (vs. rule-of-thumb methods.)
2. Scientific selection of workers for each job.
3. Cooperation between management and workers.
4. More equal division of responsibilities between management and workers.

Taylor believed that scientific principles could make work not only more efficient, but also less physically demanding, and that carefully-selected workers could, and should be given more responsibility.

Henri Fayol—Principles of Organization

Based on his personal experience, Fayol developed what he referred to as *principles of organization*, for guiding how workers should be managed. He proposed 14 principles that he felt could be taught, not only in companies, but in schools and universities:

1. Division of labor—specialization makes workers more efficient.
2. Authority—give managers the right to give orders.
3. Discipline—workers must respect and obey the company's rules.
4. Unity of command—each worker should have only one boss.

5. Unity of direction—activities with the same goal should have the same leader.

6. Subordination—of the interests of individuals to those of the company.

7. Remuneration—workers should be paid fair wages.

8. Centralization—decisions should be made at optimal levels in the company.

9. Scalar chain—communication should follow the chain of command.

10. Order—people and materials must be in the right places at the right times.

11. Equity—workers should be treated fairly.

12. Stability of tenure—ensure that replacements to fill vacancies are timely.

13. Initiative—giving workers responsibility increases effort and initiative.

14. Esprit de corps—promoting team spirit builds harmony and unity.

Like Taylor, Fayol believed his principles were universal: they could apply to *any* organization.

Max Weber—Bureaucracy

Weber's ideal organization, which he called "bureaucracy," was based on four principles:

1. Division of labor—specialization makes workers more efficient.

2. Formal selection procedures—for consistency in choosing workers.

3. Detailed rules and regulations—to ensure discipline and order.

4. Impersonal relationships—between managers and work-
    ers, to ensure fairness.

Although fewer in number, Weber's guidelines are similar to
Fayol's principles, and both still offer good advice for managers.

It's ironic that Weber coined the word "bureaucracy" to represent his ideal organization, but the term has come to represent
almost the opposite. Today, referring to an organization as a bureaucracy is demeaning; it implies hierarchy and inefficiency.

TYPE 2—THE SOCIAL NATURE OF ORGANIZATIONS (1930-1960)

Sometimes called the "human-relations" school of thought,
these theorists believed the way organizations were structured
could have major influences on the way employees would feel
about their organizations, and on how they would behave. Three
of the most prominent theorists of this era were:

Elton Mayo—The Hawthorne Studies

An extended series of studies at Western Electric's
Hawthorne Works were designed to examine the effect of light
levels on the productivity of workers. Initially assuming that increasing light levels in work areas would increase productivity,
and that decreasing light levels would reduce productivity, industrial engineers found the results to be considerably different
than expected.

Whereas increased light levels *did* lead to increased productivity as expected, engineers were confounded to learn that *decreasing* light levels had the same effect—they also increased
productivity. So they hired Harvard psychologist Elton Mayo to
find out why.

After several years study, Mayo concluded that social norms, not physical working conditions, were what determined productivity. More important than the physical workplace were factors like peer pressure, work-group dynamics, employee attitudes, how workers felt about their managers.

Chester Barnard—Cooperative Systems

In his book, *The Functions of the Executive,* Chester Barnard, an executive with AT&T, argued that organizations are cooperative systems and, as such, should encourage managers to take a different view of authority. Rather than the traditional top-down perspective, the amount of authority granted should depend on the response of the subordinate. Barnard believed every worker should be allowed as much authority as he/she could handle.

He also promoted the view that a manager's primary responsibilities should be facilitating communication and inspiring the efforts of workers; not command and control.

Douglas McGregor—Theory X—Theory Y

His studies of managers in organizations led McGregor to believe that every manager has either a negative or positive bias toward workers, depending on how he feels about people, in general.

Theory X (negative) managers assume:

1. People don't like to work, and will avoid it when they can.

2. Since they don't like work, people have to be threatened with punishment.

3. People will shirk their responsibilities wherever possible.

4. Workers have little ambition, and are mostly concerned with their job security.

Theory Y (positive) managers believe:
1. People view work as natural and necessary.
2. They will be self-directed and self-motivated when committed to a goal.
3. Most people can accept, and may even seek responsibility.
4. Most people—not just managers—are capable of making good decisions.

Whereas Theory X was once the dominant viewpoint, today most organization realize that Theory Y management is more likely to lead to higher levels of employee satisfaction.

TYPE 3—THE CONTINGENCY APPROACH (1960-1975)

Eventually it became apparent that, although the Type 1 and Type 2 approaches were useful, they were not truly universal; there was no single set of principles that would work in every situation. That's because organizations are heterogeneous—there are no two alike—so what works for one will not necessarily be effective in another. In other words, what will work is contingent on the circumstances. Three researchers led this school of thought:

Herbert Simon—The Situation and its Underlying Conditions

Simon began arguing against Type 1 thinking as early as the 1940s, suggesting, instead, that a contingency approach would be more appropriate. He argued that the only way to know what was likely to work would depend on the organization, itself, and the conditions under which it operated.

But it took years for his ideas to gain support, so Type 1 and Type 2 approaches continued to dominate organizational thinking until the 1960s.

Daniel Katz and Robert Kahn— Adapting to a Changing Environment

Type 1 and 2 theories were based on the assumption that an organization could be a closed system: that it could, if desired, completely control its own destiny. Ford Motor, for example, at one time attempted to control its supplies of raw materials by owning iron ore mines and rubber plantations, as well as its own glass factory and steel foundries.

But Katz and Kahn suggested that, no matter how hard a company might try to be a closed system, it would still be dependent on the external environment, which could affect the company in ways that are beyond its control. And because an organization has no control over its external environment and the changes it brings, Katz and Kahn argue that they are *open* systems. And as open systems, organizations have to be able to *adapt* to that environment, and to the need for change.

Both Simon's and Katz and Kahn's perspectives emphasized the idea of contingencies: what an organization has to deal with depends on the situation at any given time. So they have to be flexible, adaptable, and able to respond to changing conditions, and what works for one organization will not necessarily be effective for another.

TYPE 4—THE POLITICAL NATURE OF ORGANIZATIONS (1975-PRESENT)

Whereas it is human nature to think logically, organizational decisions are often based on something other than logic. And because they aren't logical they are unpredictable, in the sense that they may not be the decisions we'd expect. Type 4 theorists focused on decision-making in organizations; more specifically, decisions made in non-rational ways.

James March and Herbert Simon— Bounded Rationality and Satisficing

Taking into consideration the human limitations of people, March and Simon advanced the theory that most of our decisions will *not* be rational, nor will they be optimal. Optimal decisions require us to consider *all* the possible alternatives for solving a problem, then to select the *best* of those alternatives. But our rationality is limited, or "bounded," by the fact that we are only able to think about a small number of ideas at a time—no more than seven, and fewer than that for most of us.

Called *bounded rationality,* this limitation makes it impossible for us to consider *all* the possible alternatives in most situations. But there's usually an additional limitation: we seldom have enough *time* to consider more than just a few alternatives. As a result, we usually only look at possible solutions until we come to one that will solve the problem.

In that situation, we don't optimize, by choosing the *best* solution; we *satisfice,* by settling for the first solution we find that is "good enough." And that's the way most of our decisions are likely to be made; they aren't the best solutions, but they're good enough to do the job.

Jeffrey Pfeffer—Self-Interest and Power Coalitions

Pfeffer suggests *self-interest i*s another reason people in organizations don't make rational decisions. We'd like to think that every person in the organization is working toward the same set of goals: those that are important to the success of the organization.

But Pfeffer reminds us there are many different groups of people in an organization, and every group is likely to have its own agenda and its own goals. And unfortunately some of those agendas and goals may not be consistent with the organization's goals. Not only that, but groups often see themselves in competition with other groups: competing for resources and recognition.

When that happens, what the organization does, and how it does are likely to be influenced more by what's best for one part of the organization than what's best for the organization as a whole. As a result, the entire organization is held hostage by the self-interests of those who hold the most power, and the rest of the organization pays the price.

That's why Type 4 theorists warn us that decision-making in organizations is more likely to be self-serving and political, than it is to be rational, optimal, or logical.

SUMMARY

Over the years, human resource theories have been strongly influenced by organizational theories. Those theories initially focused on trying to develop universal principles of management; guidelines that would apply to any organization in any situation. They concentrated on how to structure an organization, and what kinds of policies and procedures would be needed to guide management in achieving organizational efficiency.

Then the focus shifted from organizations to people; to the human side of organizations. Theorists studied the effects of organizational culture; how workers felt about each other, how they felt about their managers, and how managers viewed their workers.

A third school of thought suggested that, since no two organizations are exactly alike, the universal principles approach wasn't sufficient. This was further complicated by the perspective that organizations are *not* closed systems, as previously believed; systems that allowed them to control their own destinies. They are, in fact, open systems and, as such, are affected by a constantly-changing external environment. Therefore, what works best will be contingent: depending on each organization and what's going on in its external environment.

More recently, organization theorists studying decision-making found that decisions in organizations are seldom made logically or rationally. They are, instead, affected by the power of various groups within the organization, and by human limitations that only allow us to consider a few alternatives at a time. As a result most decisions in organizations, rather than rational or logical, are likely to be less than optimal, and many of them political, as well.

So what's the primary message from this chapter? Which school of thought should we favor? Just how should we go about managing human resources?

It seems to me there is value in each of the four approaches, so we should keep the major aspects of all of them in mind.

Whereas neither Fayol's nor Weber's principles turned out to be universal, both offer useful guidelines for managers, and Taylor's approach to job design has probably had a greater impact on world-wide productivity than any other single factor, and continues to be, even today.

The importance of understanding the social nature of organizations has grown ever more visible, and the ideas of Mayo, Barnard, and McGregor continue to offer good advice for managers.

The fact that our organizations operate in an external environment they can't control makes the advice of Simon, Katz and Kahn, on contingency management in the face of constant change, increasingly valuable.

But most important, we should never lose sight of the fact that organizations are people, and they are run by people, all of whom are self-interested, to one degree or another. And, as people, we have human limitations on our ability to process information, which makes our decision-making sub-optimal, at best. What does all of this mean?

The theories of March, Simon, and Pfeffer should serve as constant reminders that those shortcomings mean most of the decisions made in organizations are likely to be less than perfect, and many of them are likely to be political, as well.

Note: Much of the discussion in this chapter is based on Chapter 2 of Stephen Robbins' *Organization Theory: Structure, Design, and Applications,* 3rd Edition.

PART II

STAFFING

This part describes what I consider the primary function of human resource management: staffing. Effective staffing requires, first, an understanding of the human resource needs of the organization, then knowledge and experience in locating, attracting, and selecting people who have the qualifications to meet those needs.

The chapters in this section discuss planning human resource needs, recruiting qualified candidates, both from inside and outside the organization, then selecting the candidates who best meet the organization's needs and fit with its culture.

| 5 | **PLANNING** |

*"It is thrifty to prepare today
for the wants of tomorrow."*
(Aesop, circa 550 B.C.)

The first step in staffing an organization is determining what knowledge, skills, and capabilities it will need. Those needs, of course, will depend on what the organization intends to do; why it exists; what is its purpose. For that information we have to turn to the organization's strategic plan.

STRATEGIC PLANNING

A strategic plan is an organization's plan for the future, outlining *what* the organization will do (What will be its mission?) for *whom* it will do that (Who will be its customers or clients?) and *how* it will do it (What will be its distinctive competence?)

When it comes to selecting people, the most important part of strategic planning is the *how*, because that determines what kinds of knowledge, skills, and capabilities will be necessary to satisfy the organization's customers and accomplish its mission.

Of course knowledge, skills, and capabilities come in the form of *people*, more precisely, their qualifications. So the first step in people planning is determining what qualifications will be needed, in terms of what the organization intends to do in the future, not what it has done in the past. And that may show that some existing jobs will no longer be necessary, and some new jobs will need to be developed.

An additional consideration should be the effect that turn-over—through resignation, retirement, or death—is likely to have on staffing needs. Although some types of attrition are fairly predictable, the rate of turnover should be carefully moni-tored, so we can detect any changes in historic trends, and assess how they are likely to affect future staffing levels. Then our es-timates of future staffing needs can be increased by the expected turnover.

JOB DESIGN

To ensure the most effective use of resources, specifically people and time, every job should be designed with two things in mind: organizational effectiveness, and employee satisfaction. That means every job should be designed to:

- help achieve one or more of the organization's goals, and
- consider the people who will be doing the job, including:
  - their capabilities,
  - individual performance and productivity,
  - ergonomics (human engineering,)
  - the quality of work life   - job satisfaction,
                               - opportunity,
                               - anxiety and stress.

Job Descriptions

A job description is a written outline of what a job entails, in terms of major responsibilities, and the qualifications needed to do it successfully, including:

- the job's title,
- a statement of the job's major duties and responsibilities,

- qualifications required: - education,
                            - experience,
                            - knowledge,
                            - skills,
                            - equipment or technology expertise
                            - physical demand required (some jobs.)

Job descriptions are essential to:

- recruiting,
- selection,
- training,
- compensation,
- career development.

Therefore, they must be clearly-written, specific, current, and must outline the factors that are most important for success in the job

Job Responsibilities

It's important here to clarify the difference between a job description and job responsibilities.

The primary purpose of a job description is to outline the qualifications for hiring, promoting, and compensating workers.

Job responsibilities, on the other hand, are the things a person is assigned to do, once placed in the job.

Whereas the job description will rarely change, the job's responsibilities may change from week to week, day to day, or even hour to hour.

And although the job description was used to help determine the person's starting wage, future compensation will be based on evaluation of his/her performance in carrying out job responsibilities.

STAFFING LEVELS

One of the most important considerations in planning is balancing actual staff levels with the organization's needs.

A good policy in staffing is never overstaff. As managers, we should *never*, at any time, have more people than we need. The best way to do that is by *under*staffing: deliberately having *fewer* people than we need.

I realize that's counter-intuitive to traditional management thinking, which is to always ask for *more* than we need. But overstaffing guarantees wasted time and talent, reduced efficiency, and increased costs, not to mention a higher risk of future layoffs.

Staffing levels directly affect job security, and employees' perception of their job security is one of the most important factors in their morale, and loyalty to the company, which both influence employee turnover.

So the advantages of understaffing are: increased efficiency, reduced costs, lower employee turnover, less risk of future layoffs, greater job security, higher morale, and increased employee loyalty.

Of course there's a disadvantage, too: the potential for lost opportunities. Understaffing means there will seldom be people with time on their hands; nobody available for unplanned projects. But that's the purpose of priorities.

It's a fact of organizational life that we seldom, if ever, have enough time and resources to do everything we'd like to do, no matter how heavily we're staffed. And we get around that by assigning priorities to our projects; we list them in order of their importance. Then we work on them in that order, realizing that it will take longer to get to the lower the priority projects, and there is a higher the risk we'll never get to some of them.

Then, when an unexpected opportunity (aren't all opportunities somewhat unexpected?) comes along, we can compare it with our priority list, and assess just how important it appears when compared with our other projects. If it has great potential, we can work it into our list by bumping other projects that seem less important by comparison.

Prioritization adds discipline to planning, and helps make sure we don't take on every opportunity that comes along; only those that are important enough to replace something else on the list.

So understaffing can have significant benefits, including eliminating slack time, keeping us focused on what's most important to the organization, and reducing the risk of future layoffs or downsizing.

SUMMARY

Once an organization has developed a strategic plan—a plan for its future—it must determine what kinds of resources will be necessary to implement the plan. First among those resources are people; their knowledge, skills, and capabilities will be a key to the success of the plan.

So the first step in implementing the plan is determining exactly what kinds of jobs the organization will need in the future, and the qualifications necessary for the people who will fill them.

The next step is deciding how many people will be needed in each of those jobs, making sure we deliberately understaff.

Then we should review the organization's current *job descriptions* to determine which of the necessary jobs already exist, and how many current employees are qualified to fill them.

Next, any jobs that are not currently covered by job descriptions should be designed, and job descriptions written, and current employees should be surveyed to see how many, if any, are qualified to fill them.

The remainder—the number of jobs that cannot be filled by current employees—represents the staffing needs of the organization's strategic plan.

6	RECRUITING

"There is something that is much more scarce,
something rarer than ability,
it is the ability to recognize ability."
(Robert Half, (1918-2001)

Assessing the organization's human resource needs should have given us a good idea of how many jobs need to be filled, as well as the number of people needed to fill them, and job descriptions should have clarified the qualifications for each job. The next step is recruiting: locating qualified candidates for those jobs.

Recruiting is a demand and supply issue: "How many people do we need?" (demand) and "Where can we find them?" (supply.)

Since Chapter 5 helped us answer the first question, we know how many people and what qualifications we need. The first steps in answering the supply question are finding out *how many* qualified candidates there are, and *where* they are.

A fundamental consideration in recruiting is *scarcity*—how many qualified candidates there are (supply,) and how many companies are looking for them (demand.) When supply is greater than the demand it will be easier to find candidates, and their starting wages will be lower than when demand is greater than supply. But we won't know how much we'll have to pay candidates until after we've located them, something we'll discuss in Chapter 12 (Compensation.)

Where we'll find qualified candidates depends on two factors: the organization's human resource policies, and the availability of qualified candidates.

Many organizations make it a practice to fill *all* job openings
with current employees, even if it requires additional education
and/or training. That's an admirable policy, that can have a positive affect on employees' confidence in their career opportunities.

However, there will be times when the need for a particular
set of qualifications is so urgent there isn't time to train someone
without delaying an important project. So, while I strongly support filling positions from within whenever possible, there are
certain to be situations in which it is impractical, and when recruiting should be done outside the company.

INTERNAL RECRUITING

Recruiting from inside the organization capitalizes on previous investments in recruiting, selection, orientation, training,
education, and development. So internal candidates can save the
company thousands of dollars in recruiting costs, and can shorten
the search process by months.

In addition, filling positions from within the organization can
give a big boost to morale and employee loyalty, by offering experienced people opportunities for promotion or transfer.

Promotion has the advantages of rewarding past performance, providing new challenges, offering incentives to improve
future performance, and often a chain-reaction effect of additional job openings. Transfers can broaden peoples' experience
and capabilities, and increase their job satisfaction.

When employees become experienced in more than one area,
through promotion and transfer, the organization becomes more
flexible, in terms of being able to move people around to wher-

ever they are most needed at any time; the kind of flexibility that can ultimately reduce the need for layoffs and downsizing.

Locating Candidates

There are two ways of locating qualified candidates inside the organization. Personnel records can be screened for the necessary qualifications, assuming the records are computerized and kept current.

But a more effective approach is job posting, in which every job opening is posted on the organization's bulletin boards and websites, so everyone will know about them, and anyone who feels he or she is qualified can sign up to be considered for the job.

A major advantage of this approach is that it brings people who are *interested* in the job to the attention of the search committee, so the committee only has to consider people who *want* the job.

Of course, an internal search may find no qualified candidates, but when that happens employees will at least know that a sincere effort was made to give them the opportunity to apply.

And there are situations in which an internal search should not even be considered.

One is when it is apparent that the job needs to be filled by a candidate with experience or expertise in areas that are new to the organization, such as a new technology that will take the organization into an entirely new market.

Another is when the position needs someone who thinks differently than current employees. This is sometimes necessary when everyone in an organization, or a department, begins to think alike. What causes that kind of "group-think?"

When we make hiring decisions, most of us have a strong tendency to favor people who are similar to ourselves: people who think like us, believe the same things we do, have the same kinds of interests. The more we do that, the less diverse our part of the organization becomes, which is unfortunate, since diversity is highly correlated with organizational effectiveness.

Diversity, of course, comes from hiring a wide variety of people: people who think differently, who disagree, who challenge traditional assumptions. It is a fact that too many managers talk a good game of diversity, but then turn around and hire homogeneously; hire people who think like they do, as in an example from my personal experience:

I was one of seven officers in a company that was acquired by a larger firm. One of the first actions of the new CEO was to have each officer evaluated by an industrial psychologist. The analysis included a variety of aptitude tests, psychological examinations, and personal interviews, followed by individual feedback sessions in which he went through our report, page by page and point by point.

The psychologists finished his last feedback session, with Bill, our VP of Sales, just a few minutes before a scheduled staff meeting with our CEO. Bill was late for the staff meeting, which was no surprise; he was often late for meetings. He bounced into the room in his normal upbeat style, announcing "Hey guys, it's official; the psychologist confirmed what you already knew: I'm a flake. But he said that's ok, because you guys need me!"

As it turned out, the psychologist had found the other six of us to be exactly the same personality-type (INTJs on the Myers-Briggs evaluation,) and Bill was the oddball, the outlier—an ENTP—just about the exact opposite of the rest of us. We, of course, had long ago recognized that he was different. Whereas we were all pretty buttoned-down, organized, logical and predictable, he was exactly the opposite and, from our perspective, a flake. Oh, he was good at his job; he just did things differently.

But the psychologist's assessment of us as a group was what really got our attention. He said, "Just about every time you've promoted or hired an officer, you've cloned yourselves; you've hired someone who's exactly like you." On reflection, that became apparent to us. All of us except Bill were analytical people, either engineers or accountants, while Bill was a sales-type, a promoter and people-person.

That experience has affected my hiring decisions ever since. I now make a conscious effort to hire people based on their qualifications and attitudes, and consciously avoid leaning toward people because they think like me.

But an important benefit of internal recruiting is that it often creates additional openings—positions vacated by people being promoted or transferred—that become opportunities for additional promotions and transfers; a cascading effect.

EXTERNAL RECRUITING

Sometimes jobs cannot be filled from within the organization, either because an internal search has been unsuccessful, or has been ruled out. Then we have to expand the search outside the organization, which brings up the question, "At what level will we need to search?" or, "How wide will we have to cast our net?"

Recruiting Area

The level of the search will depend on the scarcity of people with the necessary qualifications, and how far we'll have to go to find them. Again, it's a supply and demand issue: where are the people we need, how many of them are available, and how many other companies will be competing to hire them.

In general, the higher the required qualifications (i.e., the more education, experience, knowledge, and skills are required,) the smaller the number of people who have them, and the farther we'll have to search to find them. In other words, the higher the level of qualifications, the greater the distance we'll have to go to find them, and distance is money; the greater the distance, the more it will cost, and the longer it is likely to take.

For low-qualification, entry-level jobs, we usually won't have to go far to find candidates, since jobs that don't require much skill can be filled by almost anyone, so candidates can usually be found locally, and quickly.

Filling technical jobs, and those requiring trade skills, will usually require expanding the recruiting area, while executive jobs will likely call for national or international recruiting.

That said, distance can be modified by population. Large cities, with high-density population areas will usually have higher concentrations of qualified candidates, making distance less of a factor for organizations that are located in those areas.

Sources of Candidates

Knowing the best sources for each kind of job search can help reduce the time and effort required to locate qualified candidates.

Employment Applications—are a source of candidates available to every organization. Although the percentage of applicants that qualify for upper-level jobs may be low, this can be an excellent source for entry-level job candidates. And unsolicited applications—those that are not in response to job advertisements—can be good indicators of an applicant's initiative/desire

The more solid the organization's reputation as an employer, the greater the number of unsolicited applications it is likely to receive, including some from higher-level applicants.

Employee Referrals—are an excellent source of higher-quality candidates, particularly where attitude and work-ethic are concerns. Most people will not recommend someone unless they are confident that person will reflect well on them. And whenever one of their referrals is hired, the person who gave the referral has a strong incentive to monitor the new employee's performance.

There are two potential downsides to referrals. First, they may tend more to be more like clones of current employees than people with diverse interests and ideas. But then a new employee who thinks like a good employee isn't all bad.

The second potential problem is that when two employees are close friends, whatever happens to one affects them both. Then it can be doubly demoralizing if one of them is passed over for a promotion, receives an unfavorable performance evaluation, is disciplined, or laid off. The effects can be even more damaging if the two are relatives, although some companies have policies that prohibit hiring relatives.

However, unsolicited applications and referrals can significantly reduce search costs, and substantially shorten the time it takes to fill jobs.

Public Employment Agencies—Their primary purpose is to find jobs for unemployed workers, so they maintain large databases of candidates and their qualifications, most of whom are immediately available for work. These agencies can save time and money, by screening applicants for qualifications, testing them psychologically, and for aptitude, and providing wage surveys to guide compensation decisions. Usually all of those services are provided at no cost to client companies.

An additional benefit of public employment agencies is that if a new hire doesn't work out, the agency takes care of the entire process of removing that person and sending a replacement. That relieves the company from any of the liability that's often part of firing an employee.

Private Employment Agencies—are similar to public agencies, in the sense that they maintain data bases of people who are looking for jobs, and their qualifications, but they differ by the types of people they have on file. Their clients are not necessarily unemployed, but may also include people who are currently employed while looking for different jobs.

Since they charge for their services, usually as a percentage of the employee's first-year wages, these agencies are likely to represent mainly candidates for higher-paying jobs, and some may specialize in certain types of jobs.

Advertising—is one of the most popular ways of locating qualified candidates. Classified ads in newspapers, trade publications, or professional journals all have their own advantages.

Newspapers reach larger audiences, but their ads are likely to attract a high percentage of responses from unqualified candidates. And it's important to understand that the cost of advertising can vary considerably, depending on the number of subscribers, the day of the week, and the size of the ad.

Advertising in trade publications and professional journals is likely to be more effective than newspapers, because they target audiences that include more people who are likely to have the unique qualifications the company is looking for.

But unlike newspapers, which are published daily, trade publications and professional journals are normally published monthly, or quarterly, therefore they take considerably longer to reach the desired audience.

An important consideration in recruiting advertising is a policy of responding to *every* application an ad attracts. A timely, straightforward response is not only common courtesy, it will also reflect on your organization's reputation. People seldom forget how they were treated by an organization, particularly in a job search. But unfortunately very few firms respond to the many applicants who don't make their final cut.

However, other companies' shortcomings can be a significant advantage for your organization. As a human resource executive, I frequently heard, from former applicants, things like, "I've applied to dozens [sometimes it's "hundreds"] of employment ads, and yours is the *only* company that ever responded." You can be sure the person who took the trouble to tell me that has probably repeated that same story to everyone within her reach, and we all know that word-of-mouth can be the best publicity money can't buy.

Executive Search Firms—often referred to as "headhunters," these firms search for candidates with the precise quailfications you need. Since their services are quite expensive, they are usually only hired for high-level executives and highly-qualified specialists. Their fees typically run somewhere around one third of the candidate's first-year compensation package, including salary, benefits, perquisites, and incentives, and may also include the search firm's expenses, easily bringing the total cost of finding a qualified candidate to six figures.

Educational Institutions—are good sources for certain types of candidates, usually those who are young and have little experience.

High schools are more likely to have candidates for unskilled entry-level jobs; community colleges for technical positions; and colleges and universities for professional and managerial jobs.

In addition, many of these institutions have ongoing internship and work-study programs that partner with local organizations to provide on-the-job learning opportunities for students. A major benefit for participating organizations is the opportunity to identify students who might make good future employees.

The costs of recruiting at educational institutions will depend on how far the institutions are from the organization.

It's important to recognize that the success of your recruiting efforts at colleges and universities will be highly dependent on the quality of your recruiters. They not only represent your organization; to potential candidates, they *are* your organization. That means your recruiters must be well-trained, in the sense that they:

- have a clear understanding of the required qualifications for each job,
- know how to interview effectively, and
- project a positive image of your organization.

One of the main reasons college-educated job candidates choose one organization over another is their personal opinion of the institutions' recruiters.

Professional Societies/Organizations—may offer member-placement services, including publicizing job openings at their meetings, classified ads in their trade journals for members seeking employment, and placement centers at their regional and national meetings.

Labor Unions—generally offer their members placement services, and sometimes maintain hiring halls for employers who are looking for day-labor, or short-term employees.

Temporary-Help Agencies—specialize in just-in-time staffing, for organizations that need temporary help, such as vacation fill-ins, maternity-leave replacements, and peak-period additions. These agencies have advantages for both employers and employees.

Temporary employees give an organization the flexibility to add employees when they are needed, and avoid layoffs when business is slack. Temporary employment is also a good source of future full-time employees, because it allows an organization to select from a pool of proven-performers.

By the same token, temporary employment gives employees the opportunity to prove themselves to their temporary employers, and working for more than one employer can help them decide what kind of company they'd prefer to work for permanently.

Employee Leasing—similar to temporary employment agencies, these organizations hire their own employees, then contract them out to organizations who need temporary help.

The employees are paid by the leasing company, in much the same manner as full-time employees are paid by their companies, including benefits. They are then leased out to client companies, at rates that are considerably higher than internal employees are paid. And they may be contracted out to the same firm for long periods—even years at a time.

A potential problem with contract employees is the perception of internal employees that these people are being paid much more than they are, for doing the same work. In reality, they aren't, since the fee is being paid to the leasing company, which then pays the contract worker probably about the same as internal employees, if not a bit less. Nevertheless, internal employees are likely to resent what they view as their organization wasting money.

SUMMARY

Recruiting is the process of locating qualified candidates for an organization's job openings. Recruiting is about supply and demand, and is driven by three questions:

"What kinds of people do we need?" asks what are the organization's demands, a question that is answered by its strategic plan, previously discussed in Chapter 5 (Planning.)

"Where can we find them?" is about supply, the question that guides the recruiting process and, of course, is the focus of this chapter.

"How much will we have to pay to get them?" is a question about scarcity: does the demand for those employees exceed the supply, or vice versa? If demand exceeds supply, we'll have to search further to find them, and we'll have to pay more to get them.

We look, first, at internal recruiting and the importance of considering the qualifications of current employees, before looking outside the organization. One of the most effective ways of locating internal candidates is through job posting: advertising each job opening to current employees, and encouraging them to sign up to be considered for it. This process evaluates internal candidates, not just by their qualifications, but also by their interest in the job, and their initiative in pursuing it.

The discussion of external recruiting includes a number of different approaches, ranging from employee referrals to leasing agencies, and evaluates their advantages and disadvantages, including a major issue: the cost of external recruiting, in time and money.

It's important to recognize that, by our definition, recruiting involves searching for, and identifying qualified candidates, but does not include the actual process of *selecting* the best candidate, the subject of Chapter 7 (Selection.)

Finally, a key consideration in recruiting—whether internal or external—should be making sure you aren't cloning yourself, or other people in the organization.

7 | SELECTION

> *"When you hire people who are smarter than you are,*
> *you prove that you are smarter than they are."*
>
> (R. H. Grant)

Selecting the right people to fill job openings is one of the most critical functions of every manager and supervisor. Proper selection brings in people who:

- learn the job more quickly,
- adjust to the job with less difficulty,
- are more productive.

Effective selection is a multi-step process that includes collecting and analyzing *information* about the job and the candidates; *testing* to confirm qualifications and develop psychological profiles; *interviewing* to discuss qualifications and assess personalities; and finally *selecting* the candidate who will be best for the position, and for the company.

INFORMATION

Information about the job and the qualifications required to fill it were an important part of recruiting, and will also be essential for considering candidates.

We will also need basic information about the candidates, including employment applications, resumes, and recruiters' reports, to use in categorizing candidates according to how well qualified they appear to be.

Screening

Reviewing that basic information should allow us to sort the candidates into three categories: 1) those who are definite possibilities, 2) those who are obviously not qualified and 3) those who are borderline: the information we currently have doesn't tell enough about the candidates to know if they are qualified or not.

Candidates in group 1 will automatically be given further consideration; group 2—those who are definitely not qualified—can be eliminated; and candidates in group 3 can be set aside for possible future consideration, depending on how many potential finalists emerge from group 1.

By the time we get to the last step in the selection process, we will need at least 3 well-qualified candidates from which to make the final selection decision.

Since background checking, testing, and interviewing are likely to eliminate some candidates, we should begin the background checking process with at least 6, and possibly many as 10.

That means if group 1 includes at least 6 candidates, we can proceed with just the candidates in that group. But if group 1 has fewer than 6, we may want to give further consideration to some of the more promising candidates from group 3.

Background Checks

Candidates' backgrounds should be examined further, to verify the information we have, and to learn as much more as we can about their performance, work habits, and attitudes. We are seldom able to get that kind of information from the references that candidates list on their resumes and employment applications, since they are likely to include only people who are sure to say good things about the candidates.

The best sources for background checks are candidates' former managers, supervisors, co-workers, or professors; people who are familiar with their work habits and work history. And about the only way we can locate those people is by asking the candidates, themselves, for names and contact information, and for permission to contact them.

So a good reason for your first phone conversation with a candidate is to ask for the contact information, as well as an opportunity to get acquainted, and ask any questions you may have about their application information.

First Step—so the first step in background checking should be phone calls to the candidates, not only to ask for contact information, but also background questions, like:

- when I ask your former boss …..."What are [the candidate's] greatest strengths?" how will he/she respond?
- in what area would he/she say you need to improve?
- why do you feel our job would be a good fit for you?
- describe the best boss you've ever had, and why you feel that way.

Second Step—once candidates have supplied contact information, each contact should be called and asked a series of questions, including:

- how long have you known [the candidate]?
- in what capacity? (e.g., supervisor/employee, co-worker, teacher/student)
- can you confirm that his/her salary was $…..?
- what would you consider his/her greatest strengths?
- what areas do you feel could use some improvement?
- given the opportunity, would you hire him/her again?

This series of questions is intended to answer one major question about the candidate: "What kind of worker was he/she?" That answer—the candidate's past performance—may be the best way of predicting his/her future performance.

Once background checks have been completed on the select pool of candidates, it's time to narrow the field to no more than 3 candidates; the best 3; those we feel should be brought into the company for testing and interviews. Why three? Because that's usually enough to ensure at least one acceptable candidate, and any more than three may unnecessarily increase travel and lodging expenses.

TESTING

Candidates who are brought in for interviews may and, in some situations, *should* undergo various types of testing. Of the many types of tests available, the most useful are achievement tests, which assess candidates' current knowledge and abilities, and aptitude tests, which assess their ability to learn.

Other types of tests that can be considered when necessary, include:

- cognitive—to measure mental capabilities
- personality and interest inventories to assess personal dispositions and interests
- physical ability—to measure strength and endurance
- job knowledge—to measure level of understanding of a particular job
- honesty/integrity—to assess propensity to lie, or cheat
- drug tests- to screen for use of illegal substances
- medical examinations—to ensure the candidates' health is adequate to meet job requirements.

Access to test results, like other personal information, should be limited to those who have a professional need to review them.

INTERVIEWING

The purpose of an interview is to learn things about the candidate that aren't included in employment applications and resumes. Every candidate should be assessed from two perspectives—qualifications, and personality—which usually requires two different types of interview.

Qualifications

This kind of interview should be conducted by people from the area in which the candidate will work, and should focus on assessing his/her qualifications for the job. This type interview usually relies on standardized questions often analytical; the types of questions that have answers that are either correct or incorrect. This can also be done through computer-based interviews, in which the candidate responds to multiple-choice questions using a keyboard.

Personality

Interviews to analyze a candidate's compatibility, or "fit," with the organization's culture and value system usually rely heavily on "open-ended" questions, the kind that *don't* have right or wrong answers.

This type of interview is usually designed to keep the candidate talking for an extended period (i.e., 30-45 minutes), so interviewers can "get a feel" for the candidate's personality, and observe his/her mannerisms, tone of voice, and attitude. These interviews focus on *how* the candidate responds, rather than *what* he says, and are usually only effective when conducted by people who are experienced in conducting these kinds of "non-directed" conversations.

Interviewers must always be aware of the generation-gap differences that may exist between *their* view of the world and the way someone considerably younger, or older, is likely to see it. Tolerance, patience, and a sincere desire to understand those differences is an absolutely essential personal characteristic of any good interviewer, regardless of his/her age.

Personality can also be assessed through *behavioral* questions, like having an applicant describe how he actually responded to a work-based situation, or how he *would* respond to such a situation.

The most important thing about interviews is that every candidate should go through both qualification and personality interviews, because even the best-qualified person can be ineffective in the wrong organizational environment, not to mention the risk of disrupting other employees. On the other hand, it should be obvious that having the right personality is of no value if the candidate isn't qualified to do the job.

Interviewers

Interviews can be conducted one-on-one—the candidate and one interviewer—or by a panel of 3-5 interviewers, each asking different questions.

In either case, interviewers should be carefully selected, with heavy emphasis on having the following personal characteristics:

- humility
- maturity
- objectivity
- poise
- freedom from - extreme opinions

- biases
- tendency to talk too much.

Overall, the most important characteristic for an interviewer is being a good *listener*.

Finally, every interviewer must be aware of the questions they *should not ask;* the kind that may be discriminatory; for example:

- How old are you? What is your date of birth?
- What is your race? What is your ethnic background?
- What is your religious affiliation?
- Have you ever been arrested? (it *is* ok to ask "Have you ever been convicted?")
- Are you married? (or divorced or single)
- Do you have any physical defects?
-• How tall are you? How much do you weigh? What color is your hair? What color are your eyes?

And remember, it's also considered offensive to include these types of questions on employment applications.

SELECTION DECISION

There are few management decisions that are more important than selecting the right person for a job. Choosing the wrong candidate can be very expensive, considering the time and money involved in:

- recruiting,
- interviewing,
- testing,
- travel, lodging, and relocation,
- orientation, training,

- legal costs,
- lost time,
- employee morale.

For those reasons, whatever extra time, effort, and money is required to locate, analyze, and select the *right* candidate will be wise investments, considering the price you pay for making the wrong choice.

And it's essential that the final selection be based on both *qualifications* (abilities: what the candidate *can* do) and *attitude* (behavior: what he's *willing* do.) Job performance isn't a function of one or the other; good performance requires both.

Qualifications

Determining the qualifications for a particular job begins with a *job description*, which outlines the education, experience, knowledge, skills, and abilities that are considered necessary to be successful in that job.

Assessing the qualifications of any candidate requires reviewing her application and/or resume, background checking to determine the validity of that information, interviewing the candidate, and perhaps testing to compare her capabilities with those outlined in the job description.

That process should result in a select pool of candidates who are fully qualified. Unfortunately, many managers end the selection process at that point, by selecting the best-qualified candidate. But sometimes they learn the hard way that the best qualified person isn't always the best person for job, or for the organization. That's why it's so important to understand candidates' attitudes, as well.

Attitude

It's reasonably easy, through testing and interviews, to evaluate a candidate's abilities (what he *can* do) and predict how well he is likely to perform the job responsibilities. But his behavior (what he *will* do) can only be inferred, and then only by examining his *past* performance.

In other words, while we can estimate, fairly accurately, what a new hire will be *able* to do, predicting his behavior— what he'll be *willing* to do—is not so easy. We can't test for it, at least not very accurately, so our best option is to attempt to judge it as best we can through interviews and background checks.

An experienced interviewer, one who concentrates on listening instead of talking, will generally be able to get a good idea of an individual's attitude, including her:

- dependability
- work ethic,
- self-respect,
- respect for others,
- dignity,
- honesty,
- sincerity,
- loyalty,
- values,
- sense of responsibility.

Having done this, the select pool of qualified candidates can then be ranked according to attitude. Ultimately the best candidate for the organization is likely to be the one with the best balance of qualifications and attitude.

With that in mind, the final selection decision should be made by the manager or supervisor to whom the new employee will report.

To maintain consistency in their hiring standards, some organizations make all their selection decisions at a higher level in the organization.

One of the most successful convenience-store chains, for example, requires that all hiring decisions for employees in its outlets be made by division managers. Each of these managers, who normally oversee perhaps a dozen stores, make all hiring decisions for the stores in their division. That way they ensure that individual store managers don't short-cut the selection process in their hurry to fill openings in their own stores. This process has reduced turnover in the organization's stores to a fraction of their competitors' turnover rates.

While that may seem an extreme case, it effectively illustrates the importance of doing whatever is necessary to ensure the quality of the selection process.

One more important consideration: if you are unable to find a candidate you feel is the *right* one—one with the required qualifications and the right attitude—or if you've found the right one, but can't afford to meet his/her salary requirements, do *not* compromise.

You should *never* lower your standards, whether it's to hire someone you *can* afford, or to settle for someone who doesn't have the right attitude, or is under qualified, just to fill the position. In either case, you'll be much better off not to fill the job at all. Hiring the wrong person is likely to affect the morale of your other employees, as they will resent having to "carry" a new hire who can't pull his weight, or who isn't able to get along with his co-workers.

SUMMARY

The success of any organization is largely dependent on the quality of its people. For that reason, selecting the right people should be a primary responsibility of every manager and supervisor. Knowing how to do that effectively—how to select the *right* people, rather than just hiring somebody—can make the difference between success and failure for that manager, for the people he hires, and for his organization.

Selecting the person who will be best for the organization requires two major considerations: candidates' qualifications, and their attitudes. Their qualifications will determine how well they can do their jobs, and their attitudes how well they can live up to the values and philosophies of the organization, and thrive in its culture.

Most managers should be able to evaluate candidates' qualifications for jobs in their area, but not many of them will have enough experience in evaluating personalities and attitudes to be able to objectively assess candidates from those perspectives.

Therefore, each candidate should be interviewed from two different viewpoints, by two different types of interviewers. Then, considering both the candidate's qualifications and attitude, the final selection decision should be made by the person who will be the new employee's supervisor.

Your goal should be to hire the person who has the best combination of qualifications and attitude; in other words the person who will be *best for the organization*. Of course that means your final choice may *not* be the candidate who is best qualified for the *job,* because, in today's organizational environment, employees' attitudes are often more important than their abilities.

People with good attitudes can be taught almost anything they need to know—knowledge, skills, abilities, information—

but it's almost impossible to change a person's attitude, as I
learned from experience:

I was reviewing applications for an engineering position, when I noticed that one of the applicants had previously worked for a former colleague of mine. Naturally, I called my friend to learn more about the applicant.

"Was he a good engineer?" I asked. "One of the
best." he replied.

"Did he get along with his co-workers?" "Yes, he
was an excellent team-player."

"Was he a good worker?" "You couldn't ask for a
better one."

Then I asked, "Why doesn't he still work for you?"
and he replied, "I had to let him go." When I asked,
"Why?" he said, "Because he was absent too often."

"How often?" I asked. "About one day a week." he
replied.

"Which day?" "We never knew, it could be any
day."

"What was the reason for his absenteeism?" "A lot
of different reasons."

"I assume you tried to get him to change?" "Repeat-
edly, and he always agreed that it had to stop. But it
never did."

Then I repeated, "But he was a good engineer?" and
he replied "One of the best."

When I responded, "I think I can change him." He
simply replied, "Good luck!"

So I hired the engineer in question, and he was a
good engineer, as advertised, and a good person—
everyone liked him—and he was a hard worker. But,
almost from his first week on the job he began missing

work; about one day a week, and we never knew which day it would be.

When asked for a reason, the response might be anything from "My car wouldn't start," or "My alarm didn't go off," to "My grandmother died."

When cautioned that this had to stop, he would contritely reply, "I know. It won't happen again." But it always did, usually the very next week. Finally, I reluctantly gave up, realizing that I could never change him; only he could do that.

And because it was impossible to predict *when* he would be available, we were never able to assign this very capable engineer to any job that had a deadline, which ruled out just about every project that was important to the company. That, of course, significantly lowered his value to the company.

Here was a person who seemed to have everything we were looking for: excellent qualifications and a great attitude. Unfortunately, as we learned the hard way, he was lacking in one of the most important characteristics that make up attitude—dependability.

That experience taught me that it is impossible for one person to change another person's personality. Although we can help people learn new skills, only the person himself can change his attitude.

A final thought: When faced with choosing between two candidates whose qualifications and personalities seem almost equal, I always remember the advice of a respected mentor: "When in doubt, choose the applicant who *wants* the job the most."

That's good advice as long as you're confident the applicant isn't putting on an act: *telling* you how badly he wants it, but not necessarily meaning it. Another approach is to select the candidate who is most *enthusiastic* about the job, assuming, of course, that you can be sure his enthusiasm is genuine.

PART III
DEVELOPING PEOPLE

This part describes what I consider the most neglected role of human resource management: developing people. While most organizations pay a great deal of attention to recruiting people, and are also concerned with reducing employee turnover, few of them seem to realize that one of the keys to employee satisfaction is how much attention the company devotes to helping them reach their full potential.

The chapters in this section discuss the elements of individual development, beginning with the value of proper orientation into the organization, the importance of training to help them develop additional knowledge, skills, and capabilities, the role of career planning in helping them strive toward their personal aspirations, and the essential nature of performance evaluation in assessing and providing feedback about their efforts.

"New things are made familiar,
and familiar things are made new."

(Samuel Johnson, 1709-1794)

The first day in a new company is always stressful for new employees. They're facing a different set of surroundings, a new environment and, except for those who were involved in the hiring process, people they've never met before. No matter how friendly the organization or its people, in the beginning it's always likely to be uncomfortable for newcomers.

And the things they need most on their first day are reassurance, acceptance, comfort and, most of all, confirmation that they've made the right decision; selected the right employer. So they should be warmly welcomed, not only by those who hired them, but also by their new co-workers.

With that in mind, let's shift our attention to those co-workers. They'll be all kinds of people, some more friendly than others, but basically all good people. Those who will be working closely with the new arrivals will undoubtedly be most interested in their arrival, while others are likely to be ambivalent: the presence of new people isn't going to affect them much, one way or another.

However, there may be other employees who *do* take a personal interest in the new people, but not with the intention of making them feel welcome. Just about every organization has disgruntled employees: people who, for various reasons, have nothing good to say about the company; in fact, these people go out of their way to badmouth the company. Although there may be only one or two of them, they are likely to do anything they can to voice their complaints, and make their presence felt.

And because these complainers have long since worn out their welcome with their co-workers, there are very few people who will listen to their grumbling. So these people are always looking for a new audience, and who could be better than new employees? They *have to* listen, right? No, as a matter of fact that isn't right; it's *wrong*. It is the company's responsibility to make sure new employees don't have to put up with that kind of pressure.

Yet if the *company* doesn't do something, you can be sure that every new employee will be "welcomed" by these self-anointed critics. Their goal? To recruit new members to their cause, by assuring them, "I'm one of the few who will tell you what's *really* going on around here. Stick with me and ....."

Of course, their idea of "What's really going on around here..." will be intended to demoralize new entrants, and make them question the wisdom of their decision to come to work for this company.

Now put yourself in the position of a new hire. By the end of your first day of work, if you've been worked over by just one of these disgruntled employees, you may be seriously questioning whether or not you should come back tomorrow. Your first day has not just been unsettling, it's been totally discouraging.

Then consider it from the company's standpoint. Think about the months of time and effort, and the thousands of dollars it has invested in you, before you even started. Isn't that an investment worth protecting? Of course it is; but how does a company do that?

PURPOSE

While you may not be able to completely protect new employees from your company's nay-sayers—and trust me, you do have them—there is a way you can short-circuit their efforts. You can make sure every new employee is welcomed into the company the *right* way, by the *right* people, in a way that shows them how important they are, and reinforces the wisdom of their decision to join the company.

That can be accomplished by a formalized orientation program; one that's specifically designed to familiarize new employees with:

- the organization,
- their work units,
- their jobs,
- their role in the organization.

Orientation should be designed to serve two purposes: 1) to help new employees adjust to their new company, and begin their employment with the right attitude; and 2) to help maintain and reinforce the organization's culture.

In order to accomplish those objectives, the program *cannot* be informal, casual, off-the-cuff, ad-hoc, or occasional. It must be well thought-out, well executed and consistently delivered, not only to ensure that every part of the process is thoroughly covered, but also to impress upon every new employee his/her value to the company, as well as the importance of the organization's culture.

It should address new employees' needs for information, understanding, and belonging, and should answer their "What?" and "How?" questions, as well as their need to know *why* things are done the way they are.

PRESENTATION

One of the most important considerations in an orientation program that should be *who* does the orientation.

The right answer is "Managers, supervisors, and executives," *not* co-workers. For purposes of consistency and perspective, and to avoid confusion, we should make sure that every new employee hears exactly the same messages, from the same point of view and, to the extent possible, from the same people.

The company's commitment to having its executives and managers deliver the program will not only show new employees how important of the program is, but will also give them a sense that they're hearing it from those who really know, and who can answer whatever questions they may have.

CONTENT

Ideally, topics covered in an orientation program should include the organization's:

- history,
- philosophy,
- values,
- vision,
- mission,
- products, services,
- finances,
- structure,
- human resource policies,
- compensation program,
- incentive program,
- vacation policy,
- holidays,

- other benefits,
- performance evaluation process.

While some organizations do not cover every one of those topics, it's good practice to cover as many as possible, since the more open a company is—the more information it shares with employees—the more it builds trust.

Considering the large amount of material covered in an orientation program, it should not be attempted in a single session, or even two. Scheduling a 1 to 2 hour session each day for a two-week period will give participants time to think about each session, then come back the next day with questions that help clarify their understanding.

Orientation sessions should be mandatory for new employees, should always be scheduled *during* working hours, and employees should be paid their normal wages for attending.

While some managers may complain about the loss of 10-20 hours of their new employees' time, you can reassure them that an effective orientation program will repay that time very quickly, and many times over.

BENEFITS

The benefits of a well-executed orientation program include:
- a positive first impression of the company,
- reduced anxiety,
- improved morale,
- increased productivity,
- reduced turnover,
- reduced recruiting and selection costs,
- reduced training costs,
- improved probability of success for employees.

SUMMARY

Every new employee represents a significant investment, in the weeks and months of effort involved in the search and selection process, and the thousands of dollars in travel and lodging expenses.

That more than justifies protecting that investment with a formal orientation process. Making sure new employees are welcomed and introduced to the company in a manner that reinforces the wisdom of their choice of employer will pay back that investment quickly, and many times over.

The costs of an effective orientation program will be more than offset by savings from the reduced employee turnover that is experienced by companies with high employee satisfaction and morale.

But orientation need not be only for new employees. Everyone needs to be kept up to date on what's going on in the company. While much of that can be done through email, newsletters, and employee meetings, in a time of major change, re-orientation of all employees may be the best way of getting them headed down a new path.

9 | TRAINING

*"I am always ready to learn,
but I do not always like being taught."*
(Winston Churchill, 1874-1965)

The purpose of training is to give employees knowledge, skills, and abilities that are needed by the company, or that will be needed in the future. Those capabilities can be obtained two ways: from outside the organization, by hiring, contracting, or leasing people; or from inside the organization, from people who currently have them, or by training people who don't have them.

This chapter is designed to guide the training of existing employees.

NEEDS

The only justification for a training program should be to meet the needs of the organization; it should *never* be conducted to respond to popular demand, or for other arbitrary reasons.

An organization's training needs should be determined by its strategies; by what is needed to successfully execute the organization's strategic plan. Strategic needs are defined in terms of resources, equipment, facilities, knowledge, skills, and abilities. Training is usually concerned with the last three categories.

Assessing training needs requires determining:

1. What knowledge, skills, and abilities are needed to exe-
    cute the strategic plan?
    - Which of those do we currently have?
    - Do we have *enough* people with those capabilities?
    - If not enough, how many additional people will need to
      be trained?
    - How soon must their training be completed? (by what
      dates?)
2. What kinds of training are needed to develop the
    capabilities we *don't* have?
    - How many people will need to be trained?
    - How soon must their training be completed?

The answers to those questions should provide a list of all
the knowledge, skills, and abilities that will be needed, but are
not yet available, and the dates by which they must be available.
For the entire corporation, this list is likely to be long and cover
many different capabilities, while lists for individual departments
will be shorter and more specific.

Then individual departments, or functional units, will need
to determine:

- *What kinds* of training will their people need?
- *How many* people will need to be trained?
- *Who* should be trained? (*Which* people?)

TYPES OF TRAINING

Every training program should be developed with a clear understanding of:

- What will be taught?
- Who will be trained?
- Where?

- When?
- How?
- Who will conduct the training?
- What are the *intended* results?
- How will the *actual* results be evaluated?

The following sections discuss different types of training.

Non-Managerial Training

Non-managerial training usually focuses on helping people learn skills, techniques, methods, and processes that will make them more effective at their jobs, and may also help them qualify for future advancement.

On-the-Job—one of the most common types of training—helps people learn through hands-on experience, under normal working conditions. The quality of training depends on the qualifications, patience, and attitude of the person who mentors the trainee.

Off-the-Job—can be done in several ways, including:
- group-training, in a classroom,
- individualized training:
  - at conferences, seminars,
  - through programmed instruction, by book or television,
  - at computer terminals.
- simulations—of actual operations.

Apprenticeships—usually offered by skilled-trade organizations—include both classroom and on-the-job training, normally spread out over several years (i.e., 4- 5.)

Cooperative training—is accomplished through agreements with high schools or colleges, to jointly provide a combination of in-class and on-the-job experiences.

Internship programs—are working arrangements between colleges/universities and businesses, wherein the businesses provide on-the-job experience and training, to complement and reinforce students' coursework. These programs allow businesses to evaluate students as potential future employees, and give students the opportunity to demonstrate their potential to possible future employers.

Managerial/Supervisory Training

It is nearly impossible to learn how to manage simply by reading, observing, and listening. It also takes practice, and the opportunity to experience failure and success.

For those reasons, most managerial training is experience-based, either on the job, or in job-simulations.

On-the-Job—this is very similar to *non*-managerial on-the-job training, in that it involves learning a job by doing it. This can be accomplished through short-term projects or committee assignments, by understudying a higher-level person, or through transfers and job-rotation. All of those methods are more effective under the guidance of a mentor or coach.

Off-the-Job—is a form of individualized training, usually involving one or more of the following types of experiences:

- case studies,
- in-basket exercises,
- management games,
- role-playing,
- leaderless-group discussions,
- behavioral modeling,
- laboratory training.

Special Training

Basic Education—Some organizations offer remedial education to fill in gaps in employees' reading, writing, and mathematical abilities. Some have also found it necessary to teach immigrants how to read and write English.

Team—to teach people how to work effectively in teams.

Diversity—to deal with issues such as stereotyping, workers' changing values, and affirmative-action.

Global—to make employees more aware of cross-cultural differences, and improve their effectiveness in working with people and companies in other countries.

Crisis-Prevention—to teach how to manage disruptive behavior.

LEARNING

Effective training requires a clear understanding of the conditions necessary for learning.

First, *trainees* must have three conditions:

- readiness—they must be mature, and serious about learning.
- motivation—they must recognize the need for the training, and the value of it.
- desire—they must *want* to learn.

Then, the *process* must be guided by the following principles of learning:

- applicability—the training must be useful to the trainees.
- reinforcement—trainees should be encouraged; not criticized.
- feedback—trainees should be constantly advised of their progress.

- practice/repetition—trainees should be able to practice what they are learning.
- distribution of learning—training should be broken up into several short sessions (1-2 hours,) rather than a few long ones.

Overlooking even one of those principles can limit the effectiveness of the training.

Finally, the training should begin with a clear understanding of the intended results: exactly what should trainees know, or know how to do, when the training is completed?

With that in mind, every trainee should be evaluated to determine how successful the training was: to what extent did he/she achieved the intended level of capability? How do the *actual* results compare with the *intended* results? And it is essential that the training results are *measurable*.

TRAINERS

Regardless of the type of training, the success of the program will depend primarily on the quality of trainers. The most important characteristics of trainers are:

- knowledge of the subject,
- interest in the subject,
- sincerity,
- enthusiasm,
- adaptability,
- sense of humor,
- patience.

If trainers of that quality aren't available within the organization, they should be hired from outside. This kind of trainer will have the enthusiasm to make the subject interesting, the patience to work with trainees on an individual basis when necessary, and a teaching style that makes the information clear and easy to understand.

It would be a serious mistake to designate, as a trainer, someone simply because he is available: isn't busy at the moment, or who can be spared from his other duties. Trainees are quick to recognize when their time and efforts are being wasted by a trainer who: 1) doesn't know the material; 2) isn't interested in the subject; or 3) doesn't want to be there.

The company owes its trainees, and its training program, either high quality trainers, or no training at all.

SUMMARY

Making sure the organization has the knowledge, skills, and capabilities it needs, when it needs them, requires planning for the future. That requires determining which of those capabilities it already has, and which are missing, then providing training that will allow current employees to acquire the capabilities that are necessary to close the gap.

Once the decision has been made to provide training, careful consideration must be given to who will be trained, who will conduct the training, and how and when it will be done.

First and foremost among those considerations is *when* will the training be conducted. It should be planned so the training has been completed, and the desired knowledge, skills, and abilities are available to the company *before* they are needed, instead of waiting *until* they are needed. While this may seem obvious, it's amazing how many organizations don't recognize the need for training until the lack of those capabilities starts showing up in defective products, services, or processes.

Second is determining *who* should be trained. The best learners are people who are ready, motivated, and *want* to learn. Don't waste training on people who are not mature, who don't see the value of the training, or who don't have a desire to learn. That doesn't mean those people aren't good employees; it just means that employees don't *want* to be trained *shouldn't* be trained.

Third is planning *how* the training should be done. Training principles that provide the best environment for learning include: the subject being taught is useful; trainees' performance is reinforced, not criticized; trainees have ample opportunity to practice what they're learning; they receive continuous feedback on how they're doing; and the training process is broken up into a series of short sessions, rather than a few long ones.

Finally, the quality of trainers can make all the difference in the success of failure of the training. The best trainers are knowledgeable, interested, enthusiastic, sincere, adaptable, have a sense of humor, and the patience to provide individual assistance. If this type of trainer isn't available inside the company, trainers should be hired from outside. Under no circumstances should the company attempt to fill in with people who "happen to be available."

Regardless of when or where training is scheduled, employees should be paid their normal wages while attending training sessions. And if travel and/or lodging are required, those expenses should be paid by the company; not the trainee.

<table>
<tr><td>

10

</td><td>

CAREER DEVELOPMENT

</td></tr>
</table>

"The spirit of self-help
is the root of all genuine growth
in the individual ."
(Samuel Smiles, 1812-1904)

The purpose of career development is to encourage people to develop their capabilities, so they can achieve their highest potential. While it's easy to visualize the benefit to an employee, the value to the employer is not as obvious. But it's easier to see how the organization benefits, if you can accept the fact that the key to any company's growth, and ultimate success, is the growth of its people. As its people grow, the company grows.

That's why developing people is one of the most important responsibilities of every manager, at every level in an organization. It's so important, in fact, that career development should begin right after a new employee joins the organization, as soon as orientation has been completed.

RESPONSIBILITY

As we discussed in an earlier chapter, orientation and training are initiated to meet organizational needs, so it's the company's responsibility to determine when and where they are conducted, and to make sure they are done on company time and at company expense.

But career development is different. It should be intended to benefit individual employees—to increase their value and future potential—without consideration for how long they may stay with the company. That's why individual career development should be the responsibility of the employee, not the company.

Therefore, a manager's role is *not* to take responsibility for career development, but to *encourage and support* the development efforts of their workers. Employees should take the initiative in designing their own career-development plans, and following through on them, while their manager's participation should be:

- understanding, encouraging, and praising the individual's initiative and effort,
- helping identify potential promotion opportunities within the company,
- explaining the company's educational-assistance program and policies,
- offering flexibility in the person's work schedule, to the extent possible,
- providing advice and guidance, when requested.

And individual career-development efforts should *not* be done on company time nor at company expense, except those expenses covered by the company's educational reimbursement policy.

While some might question the wisdom of providing reimbursement for educational efforts that may ultimately lead an employee *away* from the organization, research has shown that companies with that kind of policy actually *attract* more people than they lose.

THE INDIVIDUAL

An individual's first step in career development should be conducting an objective self-analysis, to determine if the individual has the two personal characteristics that are most important for success: 1) a sense of personal responsibility and, 2) a positive attitude.

If the person does *not* currently have both of those characteristics, or if they aren't strong enough, the probability that she will follow through on a career development plan is not very good, and she should be encouraged to delay career development until she is more mature.

But if she does have a good sense of personal responsibility, and a positive attitude, she should lay out a set of ground rules that will help maintain a balance between her career aspirations and her:

- physical health,
- emotional well-being,
- stress level,
- interpersonal relationships,
- family,
- financial security,
- retirement.

That will require another self-analysis, to determine her personal needs, wants, interests, and desires, to give a better idea of what she wants, and where she wants to go. Then it may be a good idea to seek career counseling, to help determine which career paths would be most suitable for her. By interpreting the results of an inexpensive series of aptitude and personality tests, an experienced psychologist can predict which types of jobs will be most in line with a person's interests. Most colleges and universities offer these types of analysis, for a modest fee, and many of them are available on the internet, including professsional interpretation.

Next, she should evaluate potential long-term employment opportunities, to determine which professions and jobs are likely to be most in demand 5, 10, or 15 years from now.

Finally, her manager can help determine where there may be future opportunities within the company, by examining:

- logical job-progression sequences,
- dual-career paths,
- the company's succession plan.

This will identify not only job opportunities but also what types of education, training, and experience may be required for each career path.

Effective self-evaluation can help the individual balance her career aspirations and personal preferences with the needs of the organization.

THE ORGANIZATION

For the organization, a direct benefit of career planning is the increase in organizational capabilities that comes from the increases in its employees' capabilities. An *indirect* benefit, and a major one, is the increase in employees' job satisfaction, which usually has the direct affects of improving morale and reducing employee turnover.

The organization's primary *responsibility* in career development is implementing the career-development program and its processes, and ensuring that the program is highly-visible, understood by every employee, and is easily accessible.

The effectiveness of the program will depend on how well it is supported by human resource policies, and on managers who take seriously their responsibilities of encouraging and supporting participants.

Also helpful is an organizational succession plan, and the availability of expert individual career-counseling.

Employees participating in the program may be at any of 5 different stages of career development, each of which is likely to require different kinds of encouragement and support:

1. Preparation for work ages 0-25
2. Organizational entry 18-25
3. Early career 25-40
4. Mid career 40-55
5. Late career 55–retirement

While our discussion, to this point, has focused on *individual* career development, there are also career development programs designed for *groups* of people, including:

- Management-Development—to help managers and potential managers gain the knowledge and experience that are necessary for managerial success.
- Women—to prepare them for advancement, and help them overcome barriers, and deal with family issues.
- Minorities—to prepare them for advancement, and help them overcome barriers.
- Dual-Career Couples—to help them balance child-care needs, time demands, relocation issues, and emotional stress.

SUMMARY

Career development is a process through which organizations encourage their people to work toward their individual aspirations.

It differs from orientation and training in that career development is the responsibility of the individual, not the company. The company's responsibility is to provide the program, and encourage and support employees' development efforts.

Individuals should only participate in career development if they have a sense of personal responsibility and a positive attitude.

Only then should they be encouraged to move forward in:

- designing a personal career-development plan,
- evaluating possible career paths,
- assessing their personal and professionals aspirations,
- matching those personal characteristics with possible jobs and professions.

When done the right way, career development can increase employees' job satisfaction, and have a major affect on company success. In fact, a recent study found that employees who are encouraged by their companies to develop additional knowledge, skills, and experience, stay with their companies longer. Their new capabilities not only increase their market value, but also their satisfaction with the company, and their company loyalty. (Craig, et al, 2009)

11 PERFORMANCE

*"Hold yourself responsible for a higher standard
than anyone else expects of you."*
(Henry Ward Beecher, 1813-1887)

The success of any organization, or any work unit, depends on the performance of people: individual employees. So a primary responsibility of every manager should be helping people improve their performance.

Improving performance begins with a clear definition of each person's responsibilities—exactly what that individual is expected to accomplish—which requires setting individual goals. Then we will be able to evaluate how each person is performing, by periodically assessing her progress toward achieving those goals.

GOALS

The organization's goals are determined by its mission, and success is measured by how well it achieves those goals. But the organization's goals can only be achieved by breaking them down into sets of sub-goals (a process called "cascading") for every level of the organization.

Through that process, a small number of organization-level goals ultimately gets broken down into hundreds, or thousands of individual goals, which will, in turn, drive the actions and activities that are necessary to achieve the organizational goals. Those actions and activities, of course, will be done by individual employees, and groups of employees.

That's why the success of the organization depends on the performance of people: it's *their* actions and activities, not those of corporate executives, that either will, or will not, achieve the organization's goals. And whether or not the *right* actions and activities get done the *right* way, and on *schedule*, will depend on the performances of a multitude of individual employees.

If every person in the organization achieves his goals, the combined effects will achieve the organization's goals, but the failure of just one person to achieve individual goals can keep the organization from reaching its goals.

That leads to the first rule of goal-setting: every person's individual goals must relate, directly or indirectly, to the organization's goals.

Rule number 2: any goal, action, activity, or expenditure that does not relate to one of the organization's goals should *not* be done. And it doesn't matter if it's something that's been done for years; if it doesn't relate to one of the organization's goals, it should be discontinued.

Rule number 3: every goal, at every level, should be measurable, which means it must be stated in a way that answers three questions:

- *What* is the goal? (What, exactly, needs to be done?)
- *How much* of it must be done? (The goal must be stated in numbers.)
- By *when*? (The goal must have a deadline; a date)

Rule number 4: every goal should be challenging, but achievable:

- *Challenging*—it should *not* be *easy* to achieve,
- *Achievable*—but it must be *possible* to achieve.

EVALUATING PERFORMANCE

Performance evaluation is a critical factor in developing people, and has major influences on other areas of human resource management, especially training (Chapter 9,) and compensation (Chapter 12.)

Performance should always be evaluated with a philosophy of continuous improvement: no matter how good performance is, it can always be improved, and we should always be looking for ways to improve it. Perhaps it's easier to see why that makes sense if we consider our competitors.

Serious competitors will always be trying to find ways to make their products and services more attractive to customers than ours. That means if we don't keep improving, they're likely to begin attracting customers away from us.

A company that believes in continuous improvement will focus its performance evaluation process on two questions:

- *Where* can performance can be improved?
- *How* can it be improved?

And these questions should be asked at every level of the organization, from corporate down to the individual.

Evaluating performance isn't just observing how well a person is doing his/her job, but requires comparing *actual* performance with *expected* performance. A person's expected performance should be clearly specified by his goals, which is why describing goals in measurable terms (What? How much? When?) is so important.

We can then evaluate performance by measuring what the person *actually* accomplished:

- Did he get the expected *result*? (and was it the *right* result?)
- in the desired *quantity*?
- by the scheduled *date*?

If the answer to any of those questions is "no," we should follow up with:

- How far did he fall short? (result, quantity, and/or date)
- What seemed to be the *problem*? (never *who* was the problem)
- What do we think *caused* the problem?
- What do we need to do to eliminate that *root cause*? (not the *problem*)

Too often, so-called problem-solving doesn't really solve the problem; instead it just addresses symptoms, and the problem soon reappears. But locating what's *causing* the problem can let us fix the root cause, and eliminate the problem, once and for all.

An important consideration in performance evaluation is believing that *every person wants to do a good job,* assuming, of course, that we've selected good people in the first place. When we have confidence in our people—that they're dependable—we should give them the benefit of the doubt, and proceed with the knowledge that, whenever something doesn't go as expected, it probably wasn't the fault of any individual.

That way, when something does go wrong, we can proceed with confidence that the problem is probably systemic, caused by things like bottlenecks in the flow of material or information, lack of training, lack of proper tools, or perhaps a mismatch between the person and the job.

That perspective allows us to drive *blame* out of the organization. Then, with finger-pointing eliminated, we can focus on solving the *real* problem, quickly and unemotionally.

An important side-benefit is that a philosophy of performance-improvement creates an atmosphere in which competition and defensiveness are replaced with trust and cooperation.

Of course, we may occasionally come across situations in which the problem is a person, although that's the exception rather than the rule. But when we do, it's important to recognize that it is a *behavioral* issue, which should be dealt with quickly, before it can escalate. (More about this below, under Behavior.)

IMPROVING PERFORMANCE

Believing that good people *want to do a good job* makes it much easier to improve individual performance. Good people don't require a lot of encouragement; they're usually trying to find better ways of doing their jobs, on their own.

The two major factors affecting individual performance are peoples' abilities and their behavior; *abilities* meaning what they *can* do, and *behavior* what they're *willing* to do.

Abilities

A person's abilities are their qualifications, and generally include:

- education,
- experience,
- knowledge,
- skills,
- abilities.

Examining their qualifications helps us predict what they may be able to do, both on the job, and for the organization, and can give us a good idea of their potential for development.

Their abilities will also be a major factor in determining their value to the company and, as a result, their compensation.

Behavior

Individual behavior is largely driven by attitude, which may influence a person's:

- self-respect,
- respect for others,
- dignity,
- ethics,
- dependability,
- work ethic,
- loyalty,
- honesty,
- integrity.

Attitude influences our willingness to do what is expected, and is a good indicator of the effect we are likely to have on our co-workers and their morale.

A major difference between abilities and behavior is how we deal with them.

When a new employee's performance is affected by his/her abilities, or lack of them, we have several possible courses of action, ranging from training to job placement. Our decision should be guided by the knowledge that we're dealing with a person who *wants* to do a good job, and we should be committed to working with them until they are capable of doing a good job, either in their current position or in a more suitable job.

A person with a behavior problem, on the other hand, may also want to succeed, but isn't willing to do what the company wants him to do. It isn't that he *can't* do the job; it's that he isn't willing to do it, or to do it the way he's supposed to. In situations like this, our approach should be to tell him what he needs to change, and give him a specified amount of time to change (e.g., 90 days,) then explain the consequences if he doesn't (e.g., he will be fired.) Then, if he doesn't change, follow through with those consequences.

An effective organization needs effective people; people who not only have the abilities it needs, but also the right attitude. If they don't have both, they shouldn't be hired. If they're already in the company but don't have the right attitude, they should be given a deadline to shape up or get out.

Performance improvement is simple when you have the right kind of people. Then, all you, as a manager, have to do is:

- provide *clearly-specified*, measurable *goals*,(goals consistent with the person's job responsibilities)
- be *supportive*—"What can I do to help?"
- encourage *participation*,
- express *appreciation*,
- minimize *criticism*,
- *follow up* consistently,
- concentrate on
   - evaluating the *full range* of a person's *responsibilities* (not just the things he does well, or does poorly)
   - evaluating *consistency* of performance (year-to-year,)
   - using *measurable* criteria,
   - *praising* performance,
   - *improving* performance,
- address *below-standard* performance:
   - *immediately* (don't wait for the formal evaluation,)
   - in terms of the *action*, not the person,
   - through *joint* problem-solving (forget about blame.)

And never evaluate a person on something that's beyond his control.

PERFORMANCE-EVALUATION PROGRAMS

The most effective performance-evaluation programs are based on clear standards of performance, which focus on job responsibilities that are related to the organization's goals.

While performance can be evaluated in many ways, most companies use one of three proven methods: *traits*, *behavioral*, or *results*.

Traits—trait methods have been the most popular, although they can be subjective and biased. They usually measure several (e.g., 7 or 8) individual characteristics, such as quantity of work, quality, attendance, teamwork, cooperation, creativity, etc.

The subjectivity of these systems can be significantly reduced by using a quantified point -system to evaluate each trait. Personally, I prefer a system, in which each characteristic is evaluated on a three-point scale: 1 point = needs improvement, 2 points = meets expectations, or 3 points = exceeds expectations. It's also useful to give each person an overall evaluation, using the same three-point scale. This method can be made even less subjective if each point on the scale is described in some quantifiable form. For example, for attendance that might be:

1 point—needs improvement   absent more than 5 days during the year,

2 points—meets expectations   absent 2-4 days,

3 points—exceeds expectations   absent less than 2 days.

Behavioral methods—are considered by some to be a more useful method of evaluation, although managers have tended to resist them, because they require individual documentation, and the evaluations can also be quite subjective. Behavioral evaluations can range from discussing how a person handled a specific "critical incident," to an overall evaluation of his/her strengths, and areas in which improvement is needed.

Results—often called "Management By Objectives" or MBO, this method requires setting goals for each person, then evaluating how effectively they achieved those goals. This is a very good way of keeping people focused on what's most important to the organization, but for some reason it has primarily been used for evaluating management people.

SUMMARY

The performance of any organization is only as good as the performance of its people. For that reason, the primary goal of a performance evaluation program should be to *improve* individual performance.

For individual performance to affect organizational performance, the efforts of every person in the organization must be focused on the actions necessary to achieving the organization's goals.

Therefore, each person's goals must be directly or indirectly related to the organization's goals, and individual performance must be evaluated in terms of how well the individual achieved his/her goals.

With that in mind, the principles of performance evaluation should be:

- performance should be evaluated by the achievement of *individual goals*,
- *individual goals* must *relate* to *organizational goals*,
- we should assume that *every person wants to do a good job*,
- our focus should be on *improving* individual performance, (vs. criticizing it)
- individual performance should be evaluated from two perspectives:
    - what the person is *able* to do (qualifications),

- what he is *willing* to do (attitude.)

A word of caution about encouraging employees to do more than one thing at a time. Studies have demonstrated that "multi-tasking" actually *impairs* individual performance. In fact, people who concentrate on one thing at a time outperform multi-taskers, in terms of results—what they actually get done. While we may be *doing* several things at once, most of us can only concentrate our attention on one thing at a time.

A young lady who passed me on the way to work one morning had a cigarette in her left hand, was applying eye makeup with her right, and had a cell phone sandwiched between her left shoulder and ear. I can only assume she was steering with her knees, which would help explain the statistic that people who talk on the phone while driving are four times as likely to have accidents as those who don't.

PART IV
REWARDING PERFORMANCE

This part discusses the natural follow up to performance evaluation: how to reward people for their performance. In doing so, it focuses on the value of differentiating between different levels of performance, and incentive provided by peoples' awareness that high performance will earn higher rewards than will average performance, and that rewards will be withheld from those whose performance is below expectations.

The chapters in this section discuss the three major categories of rewards: compensation, incentives, and benefits.

12 | COMPENSATION

> *"... wages are the value expression*
> *of what the worker produces."*
> (Joseph A. Schumpeter, 1883-1950)

The main reason most people go to work is for compensation: wages paid for the work they do. But wages are only one of several ways companies reward their workers. Others include bonuses, commissions, and the many forms of indirect compensation that we classify as benefits.

Compensation is a key to attracting and retaining the people an organization needs to do its work. With that in mind, one of the most important principles in compensation is *never* try to cut corners when it comes to wages. It's much smarter to hire fewer workers and pay them well, than to skimp on wages so you can save money, or hire more people.

COMPENSATION PROGRAMS

A compensation program should clearly:

- define its own *objectives,* (see *Objectives,* below,)
- outline the company's compensation *policies* (see *Policies,* below,)
- describe compensation *practices* and *processes,*
- communicate *information* about compensation.

Objectives—a compensation program should be designed to:

- reward past performance,
- motivate future performance,
- keep the company competitive in labor markets,
- ensure wage equity among employees (note: equity is fairness, not equality,)
- attract new employees,
- minimize employee turnover,
- ensure budget accountability.

Policies—clear compensation policies are essential, to guide decisions on:

- wage rates—at, above, or below prevailing rates?
- wage-rate differences—new, vs. experienced employees,
- wage increases—intervals, seniority, cost-of-living, merit,
- wage equity—different pay for different levels of performance,
- compensation methods—hourly, salaried, weekly, monthly, etc.,
- wage secrecy (should employees be forbidden to reveal wages?)

WAGE COMPONENTS

Some of the issues that need to be considered in determining wages are *internal*, while others are influenced by *external* factors: forces beyond the organization's control.

Internal Factors

- the organization's *compensation policy* (see *Policies*, above,)

- the relative *worth* of the *job*, (see **Job Evaluation**, below,)
- the individual *employee's value* to the company,
  the company's *ability to pay* (budget considerations.)

External Factors

- *labor market* conditions (supply vs. demand,)
- area *wage rates*,
- area *cost of living*,
- presence or absence of *collective bargaining*.

JOB EVALUATION

Job evaluation is how we determine the relative worth of jobs: how much each job is worth to the company, when compared with other jobs.

The most widely-used job evaluation systems are: job *ranking*, job *classification*, the *point* system, and the *factor* comparison system.

Job Ranking

The oldest and simplest system, job ranking requires listing all the jobs being considered, in order of their value to the company. Although this can be done by one person, it is more often done by a committee. While easy to do and simple to understand, job-ranking has two shortcomings.

First, it is not very effective when evaluating a large number of jobs (i.e., more than about 15,) so it is primarily used by small companies.

Second, it does not allow for differences in the *relative* importance of jobs. For example, suppose we rank-order two groups of jobs, as shown in Figure 1.

Group 1	Group 2
Job A	Job W
Job B	Job X
Job C	Job Y
Job D	Job Z

Figure 1. Job Ranking

We can see that, in Group 1, Job A is most important, and Job D is least important; likewise, in Group 2, Job W is most important, and Job Z is least important. But we cannot see, in either group, their *relative* importance: how *much* more important the top-ranked job is than the bottom-ranked one.

But if we use a point system to evaluate each job, as in Figure 2, we can see both their rankings and their relative importance.

Group 1	Group 2
Job A (225)	Job W (225)
Job B (185)	Job X (220)
Job C (175)	Job Y (215)
Job D (100)	Job Z (210)

Figure 2. Job-Ranking by Points

Here we can see that Job A is clearly the most important job in Group 1, and Job D is obviously the least important. But Group 2 is a different story. Assuming that Job W is most important and Z is least important, we would be *technically* correct, but in reality all four jobs are almost equally important.

And because evaluating jobs simply by ranking can be so misleading, most companies use evaluation systems that are more precise, like *job classification,* the *point system,* or the *factor comparison system.*

Job Classification

This is an improvement over job ranking because, although it also ranks jobs, it only does so to allow grouping them into wage grades, as shown in Figure 3.

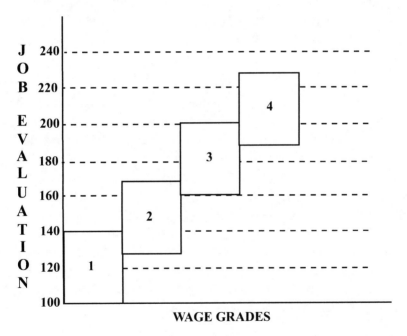

Figure 3. Job Classification

Jobs are ranked by comparing their job descriptions, then placed into wage grades with other jobs that require similar knowledge, skills, abilities, and responsibilities.

Going back to Figure 2, Job D, at 100 points, would be in lowest wage grade (Figure 3, Grade 1,) and Job A, at 225, in the highest grade (Grade 4,) while Jobs B and C, at 185 and 175, are close enough that they will be in the same wage grade (Grade3.)

But the Group 2 jobs are so close together in points—from 210-225—they will all be in the same wage grade (Grade 4.)

This system would allow a company with 150 jobs, for example, to group them into 10 or 12 wage grades, making job evaluation much more manageable.

By evaluating the differences in importance between jobs, and limiting the number of wage grades, this system avoids the problems associated with job ranking.

The Point System

Similar to job classification, the point system assesses "compensable factors" for each job, then "weights" the value of each of those factors. This gives each job a point score that represents its relative value to the company. Compensable factors usually include skills (i.e., knowledge, skills, and abilities,) mental effort, physical effort, responsibilities, and working conditions

While it's conceivable that each job could have its own wage scale, most organizations use the point totals to group similar jobs into a limited number of wage grades, similar to the job classification system.

The primary advantage of the point system is that it's more objective than the either of the two previous systems.

Factor Comparison

Similar to the point system—it also uses compensable factors—factor comparison is different in that it compares each job's compensable factors against those of selected "key jobs," which Sherman, Bohlander, and Snell (1996) describes as jobs that:

- are important to employees and the organization.
- have relatively stable job content.
- are used in salary surveys for wage determination.

In factor comparison, our standard can be the simplest type of job; one that requires few skills, low levels of mental and physical effort, minimal responsibility, and is normally done in a clean, quiet, air-conditioned environment. And example might be an entry-level office clerk.

All other jobs are measured against that standard, with differences in compensable factors accounted for using multipliers. Figure 4 is an example in which three other jobs are compared with that standard.

Comp. Factors	Eval Points	Job Multipliers/Points			
		Clerk	Assembler	Machinist	Planner
Skills	50	1/50	1/50	2/100	3/150
Mental Effort	5	1/5	1/5	2/10	3/15
Physical Effort	10	1/10	3/30	1/10	2/20
Reasons.	20	1/20	1/20	3/60	2/40
Working Cond.	15	1/15	3/45	2/30	1/15
Total Points	100	100	150	210	240

The job of assembler, for example, is similar to the clerical job, in the levels of skills, mental effort, and responsibilities, but requires considerably more physical effort, and is performed under much different working conditions (e.g., noise, dust, no air conditioning.) Therefore the last two job factors have been given higher multipliers, resulting in a job evaluation of 150 points, which would put it in a higher wage grade than the clerical job.

Using this system, in Figure 3 a clerk would be in Grade 1, assembler in Grade 2, Machinist in Grade 4, and we'd have to add a Grade 5 for planner.

Although any of these systems might be used to evaluate just about any kind of job, none lend themselves very well to management jobs, which tend to be more complex, therefore more difficult to measure.

So management jobs are usually evaluated in a manner similar to that of the Hay System, which measures:

- *knowledge* required,
- *mental* activity required,
- *accountability*, (e.g., monetary responsibility, number of people.)

WAGES

We've discussed how to evaluate the value of individual jobs, and their relative worth, but haven't yet discussed how wages, themselves, are determined: how much a particular job is worth.

First and foremost, actual wages should be determined by supply and demand. How much we'll have to pay to hire a person will depend on the labor market: what qualifications we're looking for, and how many people with those qualifications are available.

If there are not enough people available to fill the jobs that are open (i.e., the demand is greater than the supply,) we'll have to pay higher wages, but if the number of people exceeds the number of jobs (supply is greater than demand,) we'll be able to hire people for lower wages.

So our first step in determining how much to pay for a job should be to learn what is currently being paid for the job we're trying to fill, in the geographic area in which the job is located.

The best places to get that information are from wage and salary surveys: surveys of wages currently being paid by employers in specific labor markets. A variety of these types of surveys are available, from organizations like the U.S. Bureau of Labor Statistics (BLS,) the National Survey of Professional, Administrative, Technical, and Clerical Pay (PATC,) and from trade groups such as the American Management Association, the National Society of Professional Engineers, the Administrative Management Society, and the Society for Human Resource Management.

There are also employer surveys, usually conducted among groups of organizations in the same labor market, which compare current wages for key jobs that are common to all of the participating organizations.

Once we've determined the rate of pay for a particular job, we should compare that rate to what we're currently paying for similar jobs. If it appears we'll have to pay a new hire more than our current wage grade allows, we should consider either increasing the pay level for that grade, or moving the job for which we're hiring to a higher wage grade.

In any case, we should make it a practice to pay *no less than* the area's current average wage for any job. Attempting to hire at below-market rates is a practice that can easily backfire. It is likely to get you less-qualified people, or take advantage of qualified people who are desperate for jobs.

In the first case, you get what you pay for: less qualified people are seldom a bargain. In the second situation, you're likely to wind up with people who resent the fact that you took advantage of them, and who will leave at the first opportunity.

PERFORMANCE

When all the people doing similar jobs are paid exactly the same, they have no incentive to perform any better than the minimum level that management requires. As a result, the performance of the entire organization is stifled, and it's overall productivity is likely to be no higher than the lowest acceptable level.

On the other hand, paying higher wages for higher levels of performance is one of the most powerful incentives an organization can offer, and those that do invariably experience higher productivity and stronger organizational performance.

Of course, it's easier to pay everyone the same amount, but it's one of the worst things you can do to your good workers, and one of the biggest dis-incentives you could possibly offer.

Pay for Performance

Of course, a pay-for-performance system may require a different kind of wage scale, one in which each wage-grade has a range of pay, to allow for differences in performance.

To demonstrate, we've developed a wage grade with a pay range from $40,000 to $60,000 per year, that's divided into four quadrants, as shown in Figure 5.

We've labeled the first quadrant ($40K—45K) "Needs Improvement," as it's designed to include everyone whose performance is not yet up to the expected level. Those will usually be newer employees, who are still learning their jobs, but this quadrant may also include some more-experienced employees who, for one reason or another, are struggling to reach, or maintain, an acceptable level of performance.

Figure 5. Pay for Performance

The intention is that this learning-curve quadrant be a temporary location, with employees in it only until they reach an acceptable level of performance, at which point they progress to the next higher quadrant, with an appropriate pay increase.

The second ($45K-50K) and third ($50K-55K) quadrants, "Meets Expectations," are where most of the people in the wage grade—the good performers—will be. Those who have just moved into the quadrant will be near to the $45K level, while some of the more experienced people will have progressed, over the years, closer to $55K.

The fourth quadrant ($55K-60K) is called "Exceeds Expectations," and is restricted to superior performers: those who consistently outperform most others.

In such a wage grade, we would expect the distribution of employees' pay-levels to resemble a normal curve, with the average pay of those in the grade somewhere around the $50K level, tailing off to only a few people in the highest and lowest quadrants.

In this system, a person's level of compensation is determined by just two factors:

- the *market value* of the person's qualifications,
- the level of his/her actual *performance*.

The market value of any job in this wage grade determines its range of pay, and individual performance of the person doing the job determines his/her level within the range.

All other factors that might be considered in wages are taken into account in market value (i.e., cost of living,) and performance (i.e., seniority.) Loyalty to the company should never be a factor in wages; it should be rewarded by benefits such as vacation time and profit sharing.

A major advantage of this method of compensation is that it helps avoid the problem of annual pay raises eventually escalating the wages of long-term employees to where they're paid considerably more than the value of their jobs. This system only allows a person's level of pay to progress to a certain point—to his maximum value to the company in that particular job—no matter how good a worker he is, or how loyal to the company.

Skill-Based Pay

Another way of rewarding performance is basing a person's compensation on the breadth of his/her knowledge, skills, and abilities, rather than on the job he/she happens to be performing at any given time.

This system bases a person's wage on the number of different skills and abilities he/she develops, by increasing the person's wages every time he/she adds another capability. This system has proven particularly effective with teams and workgroups, giving their members the ability to rotate among different jobs in the group, and to fill in for one another when necessary.

This flexibility increases the organization's ability to move people around as necessary, increasing the organization's flexibility, responsiveness, and productivity, thus reducing the need for layoffs during down-cycles.

COMPENSATION ISSUES

Some of the major issues currently affecting compensation include:

- *comparable worth*—many jobs that are predominantly held by women are not compensated at the same level as comparable jobs held by men,
- wage-rate *compression*—increases in the market value of a particular job can result in a new employees being hired at wages that are higher than those of experienced people who have been doing the job for years.
- too little difference in pay between higher and lower level jobs, (e.g., workers paid almost as much as supervisors,)
- *two-tier* wage systems—new hires paid on a lower scale than current employees, for doing the same job.

GOVERNMENT REGULATION

Following are brief descriptions of the major laws that affect compensation:

- Davis-Bacon Act (1931)—applies to federal public works projects:
    - employees must be paid at least the prevailing wage in the area,
    - overtime must be paid at 1 ½ times the basic wage rate.
- Walsh-Healy Act (1936)—applies to work on government contracts:
    - employees must be paid at least the prevailing wage in the area,
    - overtime must be paid at 1 ½ times the basic wage rate, for:
        - work in excess of 8 hours per day,
        - work in excess of 40 hours per week, (whichever is largest,)
    - restricts use of child or convict labor.
- Fair Labor Standards Act (1938) "The Wage and Hour Act"
- applies to anyone producing goods for interstate and foreign sale:
    - prescribes a minimum wage,
    - overtime must be paid at 1½ times basic wage rate, for:
        - work in excess of 40 hours per week,
        - any extra time, even if employer didn't request it,
    - forbids minors under 16 in any interstate commerce,
    - forbids minors 16-18 in hazardous occupations,
    - requires equal pay for equal work (Equal Pay Act (1963),)

- forbids discrimination against those over age 40 (Age Discrimination Act (1967))

SUMMARY

A company's compensation programs, policies and practices are keys to its ability to attract and retain the quality and quantity of people it needs.

Perhaps the most important rule in compensation is: *never skimp on wages.* How much you pay will directly affect the quality of people you are able to hire, so it's much wiser to pay fair wages than to see how little you can get by with. Trying to save money or hire *more* people may get you the *quantity* you seek, but you'll never get the *quality* of people you need to have a high performing organization.

What is a fair wage? It depends on supply and demand: what qualifications you're looking for, how many people with those qualifications are currently available, and how many other companies are also looking for them. When demand for those people exceeds the supply, you'll have to pay more, and vice versa.

The first step in determining fair wages is examining wage surveys for the position you're trying to fill and the area from which you're trying to fill it. Then review your company's wage grades to make sure they are in that range and, if not, adjust them accordingly.

I've found that the simplest and most effective way of determining the appropriate wage for any person or job is to consider just two factors:

• the market value of the qualifications you're seeking,
• the level of performance of the individual in that job.

Done the right way, those two factors will take into consideration anything else that's likely to affect wages; things like seniority and cost of living.

Finally, pay for performance—basing a person's pay on how well he/she performs in a particular job—always improves both individual performance and organizational performance. Pay-for-performance organizations invariably outperform those that pay everyone the same regardless of their performance.

13 | INCENTIVES[1]

"You can buy people's time, ...
But you cannot buy enthusiasm; you cannot buy loyalty.
You cannot buy the devotion of hearts, minds, or souls.
You must earn these."

(Clarence Francis)

MOTIVATION

A lot has been written about motivation, most of it to help managers understand how they can motivate people to do their *best,* rather than settling for performance that's just acceptable. But in reality it is difficult, perhaps impossible, for one person to motivate another; genuine motivation invariably comes from within. While I can motivate myself, I can't motivate someone else.

The definition of *motivate* tells us that "To stir [someone] to action;" we will have to "provide [them] with a motive." (American Heritage Dictionary, 1983.)

That suggests a manager's role is not to motivate (i.e., stir people to action,) but to provide a *motive* that will make them *want to stir themselves* to action.

---

[1]Portions of this chapter have been excerpted from *Managing Strategically for Superior Performance,* 3rd Edition (O'Neal, 2008, Chapter 10), and from *Developing Leaders* (O'Neal, 2009, Chapter 13)

But let's replace *motive* with a word that's more familiar in human resource management: *incentive,* which means "Something inciting... action or effort." (Ibid.) Then we can say a manager's role is to provide incentives that will make people *want to stir themselves* to action.

INCENTIVES

In the most basic sense, an incentive is something that is so important to us that we will do whatever is necessary (within reason) to get it. The most effective incentives are those that appeal to our deepest *needs*, our fondest *desires*, our greatest *wants,* our highest *aspirations*.

That's why organizational incentive programs are most effective when designed to meet *individual* needs. The right incentives can inspire people at all levels in the organization to commit themselves to the organization and its goals. That way, helping the organization reach its goals enables employees to achieve their own goals.

When people believe that achieving the organization's goals will help them obtain the things they value most, their work takes on greater meaning, and they become more committed to doing their best work.

Designing effective incentive and reward systems requires, first, a clear understanding of the relationship between incentives and rewards. Incentives are often discussed in terms of *positive* and *negative* incentives or, stated another way, *rewards* and *punishment*.

REWARDS

A *reward* is defined as "Something, such as money, that is given... for some special service,..."; and *punishment* as "A penalty imposed for wrongdoing." (Ibid.).

A positive incentive is the opportunity to earn a reward, which must be something desirable. A negative incentive, on the other hand, is to avoid being punished, which means the punishment must be something disagreeable or threatening; something we'll try hard to avoid.

Although *rewards* have proven effective and appropriate for honoring individual performance, *punishment* is *not* the best way to deal with underperformance. That's because, when people don't perform well, it usually isn't deliberate, or because they didn't try; most of the time it's due to circumstances beyond the person's control.

Their failure may be because they didn't have the right training, the right equipment, the expected results were not clearly explained, they weren't given enough time, they were held accountable for something over which they didn't have control, they were expected to do a job they weren't trained for, or not qualified for, or for any number of personal reasons.

Whatever the reason, we should always remember that most people *want* to do a good job; they *want* to succeed, and when they fail it may not be their fault. Needless to say, if it wasn't their fault, *punishment* is *not* the right incentive.

Although we should reward those who meet their goals, we should *never* punish those who fail. A better course of action is to *delay* rewarding underperformers, until we can find the cause of their failure, remedy it, and put them on the path to success.

With that in mind, an incentive program should do two things: 1) reward those who *achieve* their goals; and 2) *withhold* rewards from those who *don't*, but then help underperformers find ways to improve their performance, so they will be able to earn rewards in the future. That way, those who perform well are rewarded, and those who don't are assisted in finding the reasons for their failure, and in correcting them.

It's important to make sure rewards are only given *after* the desired performance has demonstrated; they should *never* be given in anticipation of performance, or the reward will have no incentive value.

While any discussion of rewards is likely to be centered on monetary rewards, many of the most powerful incentives are *non-monetary*. For that reason, knowing which incentives are likely to be most effective requires an understanding of what motivates people; what makes people *want* to do something because, as we discussed earlier, genuine motivation is self-induced.

Whereas we may be able to *force* someone to do something, we can't necessarily make them to *want* to do it. *Wanting* to do something is internal; it comes from our own desire, either because it allows us to gain something of value or helps us avoid something undesirable. So, although we can't force another person to do anything, we can offer incentives that will make them *want* to do it; rewards that will help them motivate themselves.

The key to effective incentives is knowing *what* will be desirable (i.e., be an incentive) to a particular person. But how can we know what another person *needs* or *wants*? How can we learn the desires of someone else? One way is by using Maslow's well- known Hierarchy of Needs (1998:xx).

NEEDS

Abraham Maslow, a pioneering researcher in human behavior, identified 5 sets of basic needs that motivate the behavior of individuals. Shown in Figure 6, they are, from the most basic level of the hierarchy to the highest: physiological, safety, social, esteem, and self-actualization.

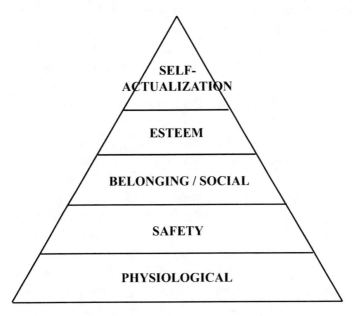

Figure 6. Maslow's Hierarchy of Needs

Maslow believed our needs are hierarchical, in the sense that our most basic needs will monopolize our thoughts and actions until they have been satisfied, and until then they will be all we care about. But once that level of needs has been satisfied our attention shifts to those on the next higher level, and so on.

Physiological needs include our need for food, water, and procreation, and until they have been met, we will devote all of our time and attention to satisfying them. But once they have been satisfied our attention will shift to a new set of needs—safety.

Safety needs include protection from the elements, from our enemies, and from illness, accidents, and disease. As long as we are worried about our safety or the safety of our family, nothing else will be as important. But once our safety needs have been satisfied, our attention turns to the next level: our social needs.

Social needs include love, affection, friendship, and the need to belong. Until those needs have been met, we will concentrate on finding a mate, having children, and establishing friendships. Only then will our attention turn to the next level: esteem.

Esteem needs include feeling good about ourselves, having self-respect and self-esteem, and being respected and appreciated by others. And only after we have satisfied our esteem needs will we move to our highest-level need: self-actualization.

Self-actualization is our need for self-fulfillment, to realize our potential, to make a contribution to the greater good, to make a difference with our life. As you might imagine, this is the most personal of all needs, and can also be the most powerful.

Each person's needs are likely to be different than the needs of anyone else, and effective incentive programs take that into account. They focus on the *differences* in individual needs, recognizing that what may be a strong motive for one person will not necessarily be important to someone else.

Since most organizations are made up of people from all walks of life—different ages, backgrounds, experience, interests, and capabilities—the employees of any organization will have a broad range of needs.

Some will be on the *physiological* level, struggling hard just to survive and keep food on the table. Others will be at the *safety* level, focused on finding a home, looking for job security, and seeking insurance to protect them in case of illness, death, accident, or fire.

Others will be at the *social* level, looking to the organization as a place to make friends and perhaps even meet a future mate.

And many people are likely to be at the *esteem* level, where their most important needs are recognition, appreciation, and to feel as though they are valuable to the organization.

And in every organization there will be some who are seeking *self-actualization*, the opportunity to feel as though they've accomplished something worthwhile with their lives.

So, what does all of this mean to us, as far as incentives are concerned? How can we possibly satisfy so many different needs?

The first step is *understanding* the current needs and wants of employees; not as groups, but as individuals. Then we have to figure out how to help each person meet his or her individual needs; achieve his/her personal goals.

INCENTIVE PROGRAMS

The purpose of an incentive program should be to inspire employees to perform at their highest level. Of course, we can only expect them to perform at high levels if they can see a clear link between performance and rewards; rewards that are meaningful for them; that help meet their personal needs, wants and desires.

In other words, an effective incentive program encourages employees to do their best work, and offers them rewards that are desirable to them.

Requirements for Success

The first requirement for success, then, is an obvious connection between performance and rewards. In other words, it should be clear to every employee "if I do this, I will receive that." That means the plan should be simple, easy to understand,

and should reward both differences in performance and exceptional performance.

The second requirement is that individual performance goals must be clearly related to the organization's goals.

Finally, the most important requirement for a successful plan is mutual trust between management and employees. The power of any incentive depends on how confident employees are that the organization will keep its end of the bargain, and deliver the expected rewards.

Barriers to Success

The success of an incentive plan depends on how well it is designed, and how it is implemented.

If the plan offers incentives that don't meet employees' needs or wants, it will have little chance for success. A good way to avoid that is to involve employees in the design of the plan; let them help determine what kinds of rewards will be the best incentives.

Ineffective implementation can be even more disastrous than a poor plan. While good implementation can sometimes compensate for a poor plan, poor implementation can make even the best plan fail.

It is also important to recognize that as soon as you put your plan into action you should be prepared to begin changing it. Seldom does anything work out the way it was planned, so successful implementation depends on flexibility, responsiveness, and the ability to find quick solutions to the things you didn't anticipate.

Finally, the organizational atmosphere can either help or hurt the effectiveness of an incentive plan. Organizational morale, for example, is an indicator of how employees feel about management; poor morale is often an indication that they don't trust management.

Management/Professional Incentives

Merit Pay

Merit-based pay, in which part of a person's wage is based on how well he/she performs, is one of the best incentives, especially for management and professional people. When good performers are paid more than those whose performance is just adequate, and when the best performers earn more than even the good ones, the average level of performance in the organization increases accordingly.

This system is most effective when those receiving it have a clear understanding of how their wages are affected by the market value of their job, and what percentage is based on their individual performance. That way, above-average performers will know how much more they are making than if their performance was just average.

It's important to understand that, in this system, every job has a maximum value, and after a person reaches that level he should no longer be eligible for wage increases. Naturally, denying wage increases to anyone, especially top performers, is a concern. Is it possible to deny a person a pay increase without discouraging or demoralizing him? Yes, through lump-sum payouts.

Lump-Sum Merit Pay

Giving a person a one-time lump-sum payout, instead of an annual wage increase, has advantages for the individual and for the organization.

The individual benefits from a large, one-time immediate payment, instead of in small increments, paid monthly for the next the year. (e.g., $3000 now, vs. $250/month over the next year.) The organization keeps its fixed costs down by not allowing wages to increase beyond the person's market value.

Merit increases should never become automatic; the fact that a person's performance was above average last year shouldn't influence his increase this year. Each employee should be evaluated every year, based on his/her performance during that year. If a person's performance declines from one year to the next, his merit increase should be affected accordingly.

Dual Career Paths

A genuine concern in most organizations is the tendency of professional and technical people to want to move into management positions, because "that's where the money is."

Unfortunately, a manager's job is more difficult than it may look, and success requires a special combination of personal characteristics that not everyone has. Consequently, many who are promoted into management positions don't succeed. And when they fail, the company has turned a well-qualified professional into a poor manager, and everyone loses.

One way to head off this situation is by developing another career path, exclusively for top-performing professional and technical people; those who are worth more to the company in their current capacities than they would be as managers.

A dual career path is a separate wage scale with a higher maximum wage—equivalent to the wages of a manager—which allows top-performers to earn as much in their current jobs as they could in the next level of management. That way, they still have the job satisfaction they get from doing the kind of work they do best, they continue doing work that is valuable to the company, and they earn as much as they would as managers.

Sales Incentives

Incentives for sales people are usually provided in one of three ways: straight *commission*, straight *salary*, or a *combination* of salary and commission.

Since they are usually self-managed, and operated independently from other employees and from the organization, it is difficult to measure the performance of a sales person on a day-to-day basis. So many of them are paid a straight commission: a percentage of the dollar-volume of their sales.

"Straight" commission means the commission is a sales person's *only* compensation. Since they receive no salary, or any other form of guaranteed income, if they don't sell anything they have no income. On the other hand, the more they sell, the more money they make, so the income of a top sales person can be almost unlimited.

While straight commission provides the maximum incentive, it can have several disadvantages for the company, and its customers. Sales people are always inclined to focus their efforts on the company's highest-priced products and services; after all that's where the big money is. But that means they neglect lower-priced products and services, and those that are more difficult to sell, and sometimes talk customers into buying products and services that are more expensive than they actually need.

Straight salary eliminates those disadvantages by giving the organization more control over what is sold, and where, and how, but has little incentive value, since sales people know they will receive the same salary regardless of how much they sell, or how little.

But companies are finding that a combination of salary and commission is more effective than either salary or commission. It offers the advantages of straight salary with the incentive value of commissions, but replaces individual commissions with a group bonus, based on the performance of the entire sales *team*.

And that group bonus isn't just based on sales volume; it also considers the *balance* of products and services sold, as well as customer satisfaction.

Executive Incentives

High-level executives, those who are responsible for large amounts of capital, who are able to work effectively in a highly-demanding, pressure-filled atmosphere, and who are capable of making the kind of decisions that can make the difference between the success and failure of their companies, are in great demand, and the competition for their services is intense.

Since the pool of people with those qualifications is limited, it is likely to require a unique package of incentives to attract and retain them.

In addition to a base salary based on the market value (supply and demand) of their unique set of qualifications, they are likely to receive short- and long-term incentives that pay significant bonuses for the achievement of specific goals. While the short-term incentives might be based, for example, on achieving cash-flow objectives, the long-term incentives are more likely to be based on reaching the company's 2 to 5 year goals; like return on equity (ROE), earnings per share (EPS), and stock appreciation. Both short- and long-term incentives are usually paid out in some combination of cash, stock, and stock options.

It is essential that executive incentives be designed to encourage and reward the kind of forward-looking planning that will ensure the long-term success of the organization. Toward that end, they should reward the achievement of the final results, or desired outcomes of the strategic plan.

One of the most frequent failures of executive incentives is when they focus too much on short-term performance, and not enough on long-term. An executive whose wage increases and incentive payouts are based on short-term objectives will be strongly tempted to do whatever it takes to make short-term performance look good, no matter what it might do to the company's long-term results.

The primary purpose of short-term incentives should, then, be to ensure the effective implementation of the company's long-term plan, by rewarding the achievement of short-term benchmarks along the way to those final results. That way, the primary purpose of short-term measurement is to make sure the company is on schedule to meet the long-term goals.

Perquisites, or perks, like a company car, country club memberships, fully-paid insurance, etc., are an important part of many executive incentive packages. While undoubtedly attractive for the executives, these perks are highly visible to lower-level employees, who often resent them deeply, feeling "If I can buy a car and pay for my own insurance, on my wages, why can't he do the same on that ridiculously high salary he's making?"

In my opinion, executive perks invariably hurt employee morale. They are highly divisive, and create a *we vs. they* culture.

Productivity Incentives

Among the earliest incentives were those designed to encourage employees to work harder; to increase the volume of their output. While we tend to associate those productivity incentives with manufacturing jobs, there are many different types, some based on individual work and others on group effort, and they can apply to almost any kind of job.

Individual Bonuses—Piecework

Piecework incentives are based on the output produced by an individual worker, who is usually paid a base hourly wage, plus a piece-rate for each unit produced above a set standard.

For example, with a standard is 100 units per day, a worker who produces less than 100 will receive only his base hourly wage for that day, while anyone who produces more than 100 will earn something extra for each unit over 100 (e.g., 25c).

This system is easy to understand, and the bonus is simple to measure and calculate, but it will only work where there is a constant flow of product coming to the worker.

There is a risk with piecework incentives: the possibility that quality will be sacrificed for speed. One way to reduce that risk is by having workers repair their own rejects on their own time.

It's also important to understand that piecework incentives can generate peer pressure from less-productive workers ("Slow down, you're making the rest of us look bad"), and they are not usually allowed by unions.

In addition to productivity increases, individual incentives are sometimes offered for reducing costs, and increasing quality.

Individual Bonuses—Standard Hour Plan

A different kind of incentive is paying a person based on how long it normally takes to do a particular job.

Best-suited to long-cycle operations—tasks that take several hours, or several days, to complete—a standard hour plan is most effective for tasks that require an experienced worker with a variety of skills.

This system is often used in automobile repair shops, where rebuilding a transmission, for example, normally takes several hours, and requires a transmission-repair technician. The technician will be paid for the standard number of hours it *should* take to repair a transmission. If that number is 8 hours, he'll be paid for 8 hours, no matter how long it takes him to do the job. If he's able to get it done in less than 8 hours, he'll be able to do more jobs, and make more money that week. Of course, a slower worker may take longer than 8 hours, and make less.

A cautionary note: there is the same risk of compromised quality here as in piecework.

Team Bonus

Team bonuses are used where teamwork is important to the quality and quantity of work, where individual output depends on the output of others, and where individual output is difficult to measure separately from the group effort.

Similar to individual bonuses, team bonuses can reward productivity increases, reducing costs, and increasing quality.

Unlike individual bonuses, these incentives are all-or-nothing: if the team exceeds the standards, everyone gets a bonus; if it doesn't, nobody gets a bonus.

Gainsharing

These plans are based on a company's commitment to share with workers the money they save the company by increasing their productivity over and above historical levels.

Gainsharing is based on the idea that, given the incentive, employees can significantly improve productivity, through more effective use of capital, labor, and raw material. The major drivers of improved productivity are employee involvement and suggestions, and teamwork.

Employees usually receive part of their gainsharing bonuses through periodic short-term payouts (e.g., monthly or quarterly,) and the balance at the end of the year.

There are several well-known gainsharing plans, including Scanlon, Rucker, and Improshare, which differ only in how they measure productivity.

Profit Sharing

The best-known, most widely-used, and most easily-understood group bonus plan is profit sharing, in which a percentage of a company's profits is shared with employees at the end of each year.

Usually calculated as a percentage of an employee's annual wage, some companies pay profit sharing in cash, while others deposit it in a deferred account, where the employee can't withdraw it until it's been in there a set number of years, or until the employee reaches a certain age, or retires.

Variable-Pay Plan

It's called a variable-pay plan because part of a person's pay is fixed, guaranteeing a certain level of income, and the rest is variable, depending on the success of the organization.

The wages of lower-level employees, for example, may be 80% fixed and the other 20% variable, while high-level executives may have only 50% fixed and the other 50% variable. In good times, everyone will get 100% of their wages, but in a bad year they'll get less: 80% for lower-level people; 50% for executives. That way, those who are most responsible for the decisions that can cause the organization to succeed or fail, have the most to lose if it doesn't do well.

One of the major advantages of variable pay is that it reduces the need for layoffs when the company isn't doing well. For example, in a year that's so bad the company can't afford the variable pay, the company's payroll would automatically be 20% lower, which would have the same effect as laying off 20% of the company's employees. Reducing wages by 20% would be painful, to be sure, but not nearly as demoralizing as seeing 20% of the company's employees lose their jobs.

Stock Bonus Plan

Owning stock gives employees an ownership interest in the company, and an incentive to do whatever they can to make it successful. As stockholders, they look at the company differently. Instead of feeling as though they are working *for* the company, they see it as *their* company. As owners, they are unwilling to tolerate things like waste, and people who slack on the job, and are much more likely to become strong advocates for continuous improvement throughout the company, and use peer pressure accordingly.

NON-MONETARY INCENTIVES

The incentives we've discussed so far are all based on some form of monetary compensation, but many of the most powerful incentives are free; they cost the company little, or nothing.

Surveys that ask workers what factors are most important to their job satisfaction have, year after year, ranked the same three factors among their top five responses: recognition, appreciation, and feeling important to the organization. Other factors consistently among the top responses include:

- interesting work
- challenging work
- opportunity for growth and promotion
- good working conditions
- job security
- being well informed

Although it's always on the list, *money* has seldom ranked higher than 5th, a reminder that the things that mean the most to employees tend to be non-monetary. Something as simple as a hand-written note of appreciation from the boss can have a surprising effect on the morale, commitment, and loyalty of an employee.

One reason money is absent is that when a person feels his wages are fair (i.e., he/she doesn't feel underpaid,) money is no longer an incentive. In fact, even when money *is* an incentive, it's only on a short-term basis. If, for example, you receive a generous raise, you may immediately be elated, but within a few days your new wage has become an accepted fact, and is no longer an incentive.

In fact, money is more often a disincentive. No matter how competitive our pay is, if we learn that someone else makes more than we do it bothers us, especially if we don't feel they're worth it.

It shouldn't surprise us that recognition, appreciation, and feeling important are at the top of the list, considering Maslow's hierarchy of needs. They address two of our most important needs: esteem, and self-actualization. And just as interesting is the fact that only the first two levels of needs—physiological and safety—can be satisfied by *money*. For the other three levels non-monetary rewards are likely to be much more effective than money.

For those at the third and fourth levels (which is likely to include the majority of employees,) recognition and appreciation for their efforts, and feeling important to the success of the organization, will be some of the most powerful incentives.

The more visible incentives and rewards are, the more effective they will be. Whenever we praise or recognize a person, it should always be done as publicly as possible. That means doing it in a way that catches the attention of as many co-workers as possible. And promotions and bonuses are opportunities to publicize the fact that superior performance is rewarded.

And, most important, we must make it clearly visible to everyone that different levels of performance bring different levels of rewards. To make sure that happens, we must have clear performance standards for every job in the organization, and ensure that the top performers receive higher rewards than average performers, and below-average performers receive less. The differences in rewards should be substantial, so that differences in performance *mean* something, and so the incentive for improved performance is compelling.

A study of knowledge workers found "... their emotions are most positive and their drive to succeed is at its peak" when " ...workers have the sense they're making headway in their jobs, ..." (Amabile & Kramer, 2010:43) This suggests that one of the most powerful incentives is for people to feel they're making progress on a project. What does that mean for managers?

It means that one of a manager's most important responsibilities should be helping employees overcome the obstacles they invariably encounter in their work. Why is that so important? Studies have shown that their manager's interest and support is a major incentive for workers, demonstrating the manager's personal interest in them, as individuals.

SUMMARY

One of the most important functions of any manager or supervisor is to inspire people to do their best; to help them want to be high level performers. In management circles, we hear a lot about motivation, and how to motivate people. But aside from the threat of punishment (e.g., being fired,) it's nearly impossible for one person to motivate another to do anything.

That's because true motivation comes from within; from an individual's desire to act; a desire that's usually driven by some personal need, want, or aspiration.

So, as managers, we should forget about motivation, and concentrate on learning what *incentives* are most likely to inspire people to act. What kinds of rewards will appeal to their desires, and make them *want* to do their best?

Aristotle classified what people value as either internal goods, or external goods. His internal goods include health, beauty, strength, physical stature, athletic ability, and virtue, and external goods are friends, money, honor, fame, and luck.

It's interesting to note that about the only difference between Aristotle's values and Maslow's needs is that Maslow prioritized them in terms of their relative importance. So maybe it doesn't matter whether we call them *needs* or *values,* both are about what people desire; what motivates us.

That's why it's so important for managers to recognize that every person's needs are different—what motivates you will not necessarily inspire someone else, and vice versa; and that our needs change from time to time, as we mature, for example, as our financial situation changes, as our interests change.

So the key to effective motivation is providing the *right* incentives; incentives that will inspire each individual to motivate himself. That requires getting to know people as individuals, understanding what is most important to each person, and remembering that what inspires one person won't necessarily work for someone else.

An important part of self-motivation is personal *satisfaction.* Research has shown a direct relationship between personal satisfaction, self-motivation, and individual performance. Furthermore, there is a direct link between employee satisfaction and customer satisfaction, and another between customer satisfaction and organizational revenue.

Those relationships suggest that satisfying employees is not only the key to motivation, but also to organizational success.

(See Chapter 17 for a detailed discussion of employee satisfaction.)

It's been said that everything we do is either to experience pleasure or avoid pain. If true, it suggests that we aren't likely to do anything unless it will gain us something that we value, or let us avoid something unpleasant or undesirable. In any event, we are more likely to take action when it has some personal benefit. That's self-motivation.

With that in mind, doesn't it make sense for us to learn what our followers value; to ask what are the things they need or would like to have? Even better, what are the things that *excite* them? Because those are the keys to self-motivation. We need to know what's most important to them so we can determine how best to help them get it. Once we've done that, we'll be well on the way to creating a culture of internal motivation.

In the final analysis, when we hire good people we owe them an organizational culture based on trust and mutual respect, and one important element of that is to drive *blame* out of the organization.

Whenever something goes wrong, as it inevitably does, we should never look for *who* is to blame, but for *what* is to blame: the *cause* of the problem. We should always assume that most people don't make mistakes *deliberately*, and they will seldom make the same mistake twice. Therefore, we should give them the benefit of the doubt, by always looking for solutions, not culprits. If we rid the organization of blame, we'll automatically encourage innovation, as people won't be afraid to try new things, because we all recognize that mistakes are a normal part of learning.

14	**BENEFITS**

Benefits are an indirect form of compensation, designed to increase employee satisfaction, and as an incentive to keep them from leaving the company.

Originally a gift from a company to its employees, the benefit package is now viewed more as an entitlement, so the organization that offers less than a full package of benefits is likely to find itself at a disadvantage in recruiting and retaining employees.

BENEFIT PROGRAMS

One of the major values of benefit programs is improving the quality of life of employees. But that, in itself, is not likely to justify the cost of ia benefit program to a company's owners. So its benefit program should be designed to meet a company's strategic objectives, including increased employee loyalty, reduced turnover, and the ability to attract quality people.

The needs and preferences of employees should be a primary consideration in determining which benefits to offer. Other factors that should be considered are societal trends that might affect employees' future needs, the amount of money available for benefits, and legal concerns.

Flexible Benefit Plans

As we've previously discussed, one person's needs are likely to be quite different than those of someone else, which means that your benefit preferences will probably be different than mine. So to maximize employee satisfaction, a company should offer a range of benefits, and give employees the opportunity to choose the ones they prefer.

Whereas traditional benefit plans provide the same package of benefits to everyone, flexible benefit plans, also referred to as "cafeteria plans," usually provide a core set of mandatory benefits that apply to everyone, plus a selection of discretionary benefits from which each employee can choose.

Flexible benefit plans have two major advantages: 1) they better satisfy employees' individual needs; and 2) they minimize the amount of money that's wasted on benefits that employees don't want, and won't value. (e.g., most young people aren't interested in a retirement plan.) That way, both the company and its employees get more for their money.

Communication

Getting the maximum impact from a benefit plan, in terms of employee satisfaction per dollar spent, requires good communication: to promote the plan, explain how it works, and keep employees informed.

Promote

We can't assume that all employees will automatically be aware of the benefit plan and its advantages to them, so it's important to promote it, in a manner that arouses their interest, and encourages them to learn more about it.

Explain

Once people are aware and interested, we should clearly explain how the plan works, in a way that ensures they understand it well enough to envision how it can benefit them.

Then the company should assist each employee in selecting the combination of benefits that will best meet their personal and individual needs.

Inform

Finally, every employee should periodically be given up-to-date information on the status of his benefits, and how much they cost the company each year. An effective way of doing this is an annual report of benefits for each employee, describing which benefits he/she is currently receiving, how much each benefit costs, and the total value of that person's benefit package.

This part of communication is particularly important, to continually remind employees of the value of the benefits that they often take for granted. That cost is substantial: benefit packages can cost as much as 40% of an employee's annual wage, and that's in *addition* to their wages.

MANDATORY BENEFITS (THOSE REQUIRED BY LAW)

Although the following benefits are required by law, they are *not* paid by the government. They are paid by employers or, in the case of Social Security, by employers and their employees.

Social Security Insurance

Required by the federal government, Social Security Insurance is intended to protect employees against loss of earnings, from:

- retirement,
- unemployment,
- disability,
- death.

These benefits are funded by a tax on employee earnings; a tax paid by employees, and matched by their employer. As o this writing, 7.65% of their wages are deducted from each employee's paycheck, and their employers pay a like amount, for a total tax of 15.3%.

Workers' Compensation Insurance

Is required on a state-by-state basis (in all states except New Jersey, South Carolina, and Texas,) to cover the cost of work-related accidents and illnesses.

This insurance can be administered by the state, by private insurers, or through self-insurance administered by the employer, but in each case the cost of the insurance is paid by employers.

Unemployment Insurance

Intended to provide temporary income for employees who are laid off or lose their jobs, this insurance is funded through a federal payroll tax. The insurance is administered by each state, but the payroll tax is paid entirely by the employer.

Unpaid Leaves

The Family Medical Leave Act (FMLA) of 1993, requires employers with 50 or more employees to allow eligible employees as much as 12 weeks of unpaid leave each year, for certain family and medical reasons.

Eligibility is earned by working for an employer at least 1250 hours during the previous 12 months. Since these leaves are job-protected, a major challenge for companies is determining how to *temporarily* cover the work loads of employees while they are on leave.

DISCRETIONARY BENEFITS

All benefits, except those required by law, are discretionary, which means companies are not *required* to offer them. This category includes all the benefits companies offer voluntarily, which includes most of those that are important to employees.

Healthcare Insurance

This is the benefit most valued by employees, and by far the most expensive for a company. For years, many companies provided first-dollar coverage: they paid for insurance that covered 100% of medically-related expensed for their employees. But in recent years, the increasing cost of medical care has made it impossible for employers to afford that level of coverage.

As a result, most companies now require their employees to share the cost of their coverage, by paying part of the insurance premium each month, and usually the first few hundred dollars of their medical expenses each year, in addition to a percentage of all costs above a pre-determined deductible.

Life Insurance

Most companies offer employees life insurance, and many pay the premium for a policy that provides insurance equivalent to the employee's annual wage. The employee may also have an option to purchase additional insurance, at his/her own expense.

Payment for Time Not Worked

This is the next most expensive category of employee benefits, usually costing at least 10% of employee wages.

Paid Vacation

The amount of paid vacation usually depends on an employee's length of service. Most companies offer something on the order of 2 weeks vacation after one year of service, an additional week after 5 or 10 years, and a 4th week after 15 or 20 years.

A few companies shut down for a set period each year—typically two weeks—and require all employees to take their vacations during that period. But most allow their employees to take their vacations whenever they want, providing they notify the company ahead of time; far enough in advance that it can schedule around their absence.

Most organizations also allow employees to take part of their vacation in one-day, or even half-day increments.

Since the purpose of a paid vacation is to reward employees for their efforts, by giving them time away from work for rest and relaxation, it is a good policy for a company to require every employee to take some vacation—either most or all of it—every year. Allowing vacation to accumulate year after year defeats the purpose of it.

Paid Holidays

Most organizations close down for a certain number of holidays each year, and pay their employees for the day off. While the number of holidays varies somewhat from one organization to another, most provide about 10 days.

Sick Leave

Although the practice varies considerably from one company to another, most allow a fixed number of paid sick days each year, usually at least 5, and some allow unused days to accumulate from year to year. But some organizations don't have official sick-leave policies, preferring, instead, to determine sick pay on a case-by-case basis, taking into consideration a person's length of service, and lost-time history.

Severance Pay

Another practice that varies from company to company is severance pay, but most offer employees who are laid off or terminated some form of severance payment, usually based on their length of service. For example, an employee with 2 years of service or less might receive 2 weeks pay, while a longer-term person is given a set amount for each additional year of service.

Pension Plans

The original purpose of a pension plan was to encourage employee loyalty, by offering long-term employees retirement income to supplement their Social Security pay.

Defined-Benefit Plans

Because these plans were primarily intended to supplement Social Security, common practice was for them to provide a payment that, added to the retiree's Social Security payment, would bring his total retirement income up to a certain percentage of his pre-retirement wage. That final percentage would depend on the employee's length of service with the company.

A 20-year employee, for example, might be guaranteed a total retirement pay of 40% (Social Security plus company payment,) while a 30-year person would receive 50%. The company would then provide whatever amount needed to be added to the Social Security payment, to bring it up to the guaranteed percentage (e.g., 40%, or 50%)

These were called *defined-benefit* plans, because they *defined* (guaranteed) each employee's retirement *benefits.* Unfortunately, the developers of these plans failed to take into consideration just how much annual wage increases and inflation might add up to over 20 or 30 years.

While they were well aware that they were guaranteeing 40 or 50 percent, they had no good way to accurately predict what a person's wages might be, 20 or 30 years in the future. So, apparently nobody bothered to ask the key question: "40 or 50 percent of *how much?*"

As a result, when that future arrived, and it came time to deliver on their promises, many companies found themselves committed to payouts that were far in excess of the amount of money in their retirement funds. Facing huge unfunded pension liabilities, they had to change their pension plans to something more controllable; more predictable, so they moved from defined-benefit plans to defined-*contribution* plans.

Defined-Contribution Plans

Whereas a defined-benefit plan guarantees an *output*—the employee's retirement pay, which is so far in the future it's impossible to predict—a defined-contribution plan specifies an *input*—a contribution. And since that amount is being contributed right *now*, it's a *fact*, not a prediction, so the company knows exactly how much it's costing.

That's a fundamental advantage of defined-contribution plans: they're based on inputs—specific contributions that are going into the plan now. That way, there's no need to fear the future, because there's no guaranteed output at retirement. The retirement benefit will be determined by how much those contributions grow between the present time and retirement.

So an employer's only obligation is to see that its retirement fund is managed prudently, which most companies ensure by having them administered by independent trusts and annuities.

One of the most popular types of defined-contribution fund is a 401K plan, into which employees contribute pre-tax earnings; earnings that won't be taxed until the funds are withdrawn, sometime in the distant future. Many companies match their employees' contributions, at rates ranging from 25 cents for each employee dollar, to dollar for dollar.

To ensure that employees' contributions will be available when they retire, most pension plans have vesting requirements that prevent employees from withdrawing funds until they have been invested for a specified period of time.

Employee Services

Most people face personal problems at one time or another, problems that sometimes affects their work. In fact, worries about personal problems are among the major causes of absenteeism and lost productivity.

Employee services are designed to help employees deal with their personal needs and problems, and help them return to their previous levels of performance.

Employee Assistance Programs (EAPs)

EAPs provide diagnosis, counseling, and referrals, for people who experience difficulties from:

- alcohol and drug abuse,
- emotional problems,
- family issues,
- financial problems.

These services are available, not only to those who *have* the problems, but also to those who are affected by *someone else's* (e.g. a family member's) problems.

In cases of alcohol and drug abuse, some companies go a step further than referrals, agreeing to pay the cost of treatment programs for any employee who makes a firm commitment to complete the program.

Childcare Assistance

Many companies offer those with young children some kind of help with the expense, scheduling, and other concerns of childcare. Although few organizations can afford the cost of on-site childcare facilities, many offer financial assistance, flexible work schedules, and family leaves.

Eldercare Assistance

Companies are increasingly assisting employees who care for elderly relatives, through seminars, counseling, information, flexible work schedules, and family leaves.

Educational Assistance

Assistance in meeting the expenses of ongoing education can be invaluable to those employees who are interested in moving ahead in their careers, keeping up to date in their fields, or simply in self-improvement. Such assistance usually includes reimbursement for tuition and books, but may also include career counseling, and flexible scheduling of work.

In terms of value to their employees, and long-term payback for the company, educational assistance is one of the best investments any company can make.

Other Services

Additional services offered by some companies include:

- food service—canteen or cafeteria,
- moving & temporary housing expenses—for new hires, or transfers,
- on-site healthcare,
- legal services,
- financial planning,
- credit unions,
- recreational/social services,
- transportation pooling.

SUMMARY

Benefits programs can have a major impact on employees' quality of life and job satisfaction, and are an important consideration when people select which company they want to work for.

While some benefits, particularly those required by law, are offered by all companies, those that mean the most to employees are the discretionary benefits: those the company offers voluntarily, not because it has to.

Although most organizations offer similar discretionary benefits, there are big differences in how benefit plans are designed and administered; differences that can have a major affect on how employees feel about their company.

A benefit plan is a major expense for any company, usually costing between 30 and 40 percent of payroll. With that in mind, it should be viewed as an investment, and designed to achieve substantial returns on investment, in employee satisfaction, reduced turnover, improved quality, and increased productivity.

A well-designed, well-executed plan will do all of those things, but a plan that is poorly designed, or poorly executed, will *not*, even though it costs just as much. A major factor in whether a plan succeeds or fails is how employees feel about it.

The most effective benefit plans are those based on a good understanding of employee preferences, and that offer benefits that are important to them. The amount of money a company spends on benefits isn't nearly as important as how well those benefits meet employees' needs.

Offering the same package of benefits to all employees is usually a waste of money. A retirement plan, for example, is one of the most expensive benefits, yet means little to most people who are only in their 20s.

The real key to employee satisfaction is a flexible-benefit plan: a plan that lets them select as many of their benefits as possible, thus letting them personally tailor their benefit package to their needs and their life-style. That way employees get the most from their benefits, and the company gets the most for its money.

Effective communication is essential to getting the most for the company's benefit dollars. We should never assume that employees know everything they need to know about the benefit plan. To enable them to make the best benefit choices, and to remind them how much money the company invests in their benefits, a company should continually promote the plan, explain the plan, and provide all the information that people need and want about the plan.

Another important goal of communication should be to build trust: employees trust in the plan, and their trust for the company's leaders.

PART V

LEADERSHIP

Whereas Part I introduces human resource management, and Parts I-IV focus on the organization's most important resource—people—this part has been written to illustrate the difference between traditional theories and methods of management, and why they are now largely out of date and counterproductive.

The chapters in this section discuss why, in today's environment, leadership is likely to be more effective than management, the critical nature of effective communication, the importance of an organization's internal environment, especially its culture, how an organization can be affected by the environment outside its boundaries, and the challenges and opportunities of the future.

| 15 | **LEADERSHIP AND MANAGEMENT** |

*"The best executive is the one who has sense enough to pick good men
to do what he wants done, and self-restraint enough
to keep from meddling with them while they do it."*
(Theodore Roosevelt, 1858-1919)

As discussed in the Introduction, one of the primary purposes of this book is to help managers become knowledgeable in human resource management, so they can move from controlling people to developing them; from managing to leading.

LEADERSHIP VS. MANAGEMENT

The dictionary defines *lead*, "To guide, conduct, escort, or direct. To influence; induce. To be ahead, or at the head of;" while *manage* is "To direct, control, or handle. To administer or regulate. To make submissive." (American Heritage Dictionary, 1983) Figure 7 compares some of the differences suggested by those definitions.

Management controls the *means—how* things are done—to make sure workers do their jobs a certain way, and is important when *processes* need to be controlled, to ensure consistency of output, or for economies of scale.

Those are usually processes in which unskilled or semi-skilled workers perform jobs that are routine and repetitive; jobs in which they seldom make their own decisions. Their managers are responsible for controlling not only a process but every step in the process, so that everything is done exactly the same way every time, to make sure the output is always the same: consistent and predictable.

LEADERS	MANAGERS
• Visionaries	• Problem solvers
• Develop fresh approaches, new options	• Act to limit choices
• Create chaos	• Seek order, control
• Determine *what* to do	• Determine *how* to do it
• Introduce change	• Maintain the status quo
• Rely on persuasion	• Rely on their authority
• Stimulate conflict	• Control limit conflict
• Welcome uncertainty	• Avoid uncertainty
• Focus on *results*	• Focus on *processes*
• Promote innovation	• Promote consistency

Figure 7. Leadership vs. Management

Leaders, on the other hand, are more subtle. Instead of controlling workers and their processes, leaders guide *what* workers do, and make sure they achieve the right *ends*. They provide a clear vision of what results are necessary, but not how to get those results. Leaders seldom require work be done in a certain way, and don't tell people *how* to do their jobs.

Leadership is appropriate when it doesn't matter *how* something is done, as long as the desired result is achieved; usually the types of jobs that require some expertise, like that gained from education, apprenticeship programs, specialized training, or experience. Because of their specialized knowledge, these workers know *how* to do their jobs, so they only need information about what they're expected to accomplish. They don't need to be told what procedures, processes, or methods to use.

So leadership is most appropriate when outcomes are important but we don't care how they are achieved, or when those performing the processes are sufficiently knowledgeable to be able to provide the necessary process control without outside guidance.

The primary roles of a leader are providing direction and ensuring that the organization's goals are achieved, so leadership is most effective when employees need only direction (e.g., vision, mission, and goals) and facilitation (e.g., advice, guidance, encouragement,) but not control. And the best leaders lead as much by example as by anything they say, or any orders they give.

A major difference between leaders and managers is the source of their authority. Managers traditionally governed by the authority of their *position:* authority granted from above. Effective leaders, on the other hand, govern through authority granted by their *followers*: authority from *below*.

Industries, and the jobs they provide, have changed a great deal over the last century, and the nature of work continues to change, making it even more important to understand the differences between management and leadership.

Before the industrial revolution, most jobs were unskilled or semi-skilled, requiring physical labor on farms or in factories, or as clerks in stores or servants in homes. In those types of jobs, workers were told what to do and how to do it. Owners and managers believed that if workers weren't constantly watched they were likely to slow down, not do their jobs right, or may not do any work at all, so they needed to be monitored and controlled.

That remained the most popular management philosophy until organization theorists began to understand how the social nature of organizations influences workers (as discussed in Chapter 4.)

One thing they found was that some workers are more effective when closely supervised, while others seem to work better *without* supervision. The first type of worker was said to have an *external* locus of control, and the second an *internal* locus of control.

Applying that perspective to our discussion, a person with an external locus of control would probably prefer to be managed, while someone with an internal locus of control would respond better to leadership.

That means organizations whose employees are mostly of the external locus of control type will have a greater need for managers, while companies that employ mostly goal-oriented (internal locus of control) people will need more leaders. For example, a manufacturing company that employees mostly non-skilled workers would rely more on managers, while a professional service organization, such as a hospital, would have a greater need for leaders.

So it's important to understand where leadership is likely to be most effective, and where management would be more appropriate. Because no two organizations are alike, there isn't a formula that will fit every situation, but it stands to reason that as an organization becomes more knowledge-based, management will become less important, and leadership more so.

As an economy becomes less dependent on product manufacturing, and more dependent on service-based organizations, workers' knowledge becomes increasingly important to an organization's competitive advantage. And, when an organization's distinctive competence is based more on what it *knows*, than on what it does, or how it does it, leadership will become more appropriate than management.

As knowledge becomes more important to an organization's success, attracting, hiring, and retaining knowledgeable people becomes essential. People who are hired for their knowledge are more likely to be self-directed, so they will flourish in an open environment, and resent excessive interference in how they perform their jobs. Making an organization attractive to this type of employee, and assuring that their work is satisfying for them, will more likely happen through leadership (vision, guidance, support) than by management (control).

Although we can continue to *manage things*, we will increasingly need to *lead people*, and one of the most critical factors in successful leadership is a leader's *personal example*. While followers may hear what their leader says, they will *believe* in what they see him *do*. That means a leader must always be aware of how his actions look to followers; how they are likely to be interpreted.

SELF-AWARENESS

Before you can become effective as a leader, you will have to be able to see yourself as other see you; to know yourself, inside and out. Only then can you know where you may need to improve.

Self-awareness requires getting to know yourself, objectively and unemotionally. Sometimes that's difficult, and it can be quite humbling, but it's absolutely necessary to developing an accurate picture of who you are and how you operate. You need a clear sense of your *attitude*, your *capabilities*, and your sense of *personal responsibility*.

Attitude

Your attitude is how you feel about yourself, and it has a powerful influence on your actions, behavior, and effectiveness. When you feel good about yourself it shows, in your enthusiasm, how you come across to others and, ultimately in your quality of life.

Your attitude can be your greatest advantage or your worst enemy, and it's something only you can control. In fact, attitude is so important that many employers, today, consider it the single most important personal characteristic when they make a hiring decision. To them it's even more important than qualifications, because they know people can be taught the necessary skills and abilities for most jobs, but it's nearly impossible to change a person's attitude.

Some of the most important elements of attitude are dependability, work ethic, respect, loyalty, dignity, modesty, enthusiasm, and especially optimism. Whether you are optimistic or pessimistic will have a major influence on your personal relationships. Most of us would much rather spend time with someone who is positive and upbeat than with people who are pessimistic and cynical.

Capabilities

It's also important to have a clear picture of your personal capabilities: the things you know how to do. They are an important part of the qualifications that will help you achieve personal and professional success. Developed through education and experience, your capabilities include the knowledge, skills, and abilities that are, or can become, your unique strengths.

While it's important to know your strengths, so they can help build your confidence, you also need to be aware of your weaknesses. We all have weaknesses, but not all of them matter. The only weaknesses you need to be concerned with are those that are most likely to hold you back. Those you will need to do something about; which is why we call them "areas for improvement."

A well-balanced person may be well aware of his strengths, and in which areas he needs to improve. If so, he should be able to evaluate just how much of an advantage his strengths are likely to be, and how vulnerable his weaknesses may make him. Unfortunately, most of us are not that objective about ourselves, so we'll need help in getting an objective self-assessment. From whom?

Your best critics will be anyone who *expects* something of you, or who is *affected* by your actions: by what you do and how you do it. They are most likely to include your family, friends, and business associates; anyone who, either consciously or unconsciously, analyzes what you do, how well you do it, where you're meeting their expectations, and where you're falling short.

Ask those people what they feel are your best points; your personal assets; your strengths. Then ask what they feel are areas in which you could use some improvement. But, beware: if you're anything like me, you'll feel hurt when they criticize you; that's human nature. And it's normal if it shakes your self-confidence a bit, and you become defensive. But remember, anyone who has the courage and willingness to do you this service deserves your heartfelt thanks, not an angry response.

I know this method works; I've been doing it for a long time. In every class that I teach, about a third of the way through the semester I have every student fill out an anonymous questionnaire, in which they assess how they feel the class is going: what's helpful for them, what they don't like, and what they'd like to see improved. While it's easy to become defensive while I read their responses, over the years student evaluations and comments have helped me become a better professor than I would have otherwise been. And there's an important side-benefit: their evaluations keep me from becoming complacent and overconfident.

Personal Responsibility

Personal responsibility means a willingness to take full responsibility for yourself and your actions. For leaders, it requires setting high expectations for yourself, and assuming responsibility for self-evaluation, self-improvement and self-discipline.

Self-Evaluation

Self-evaluation is essential to self-improvement, so each of us needs an objective perspective of how we're doing. Some of that we can do ourselves, but remaining objective requires opinions from others. That means reaching out, again, and asking for feedback from people whose opinions you value.

Self-Improvement

All of us have times when we would rather do nothing; just sit back and let things happen. But deep down, we know we'll be more successful if we proactively plan the future we want, then do whatever is necessary to achieve it. If our current capabilities won't be enough to take us all the way, which is usually the case, we will have to continue to improve, to gain new knowledge, additional skills, and/or more experience. And those are things nobody else can do that for us; the responsibility for improving ourselves is ours, alone.

Self-Discipline

People who are self-disciplined take the initiative in developing good habits: like being well-organized, arriving on time, being dependable and consistent, and making the best use of their time and efforts. And when things don't go as planned, they don't blame it on others or bad luck; they accept full responsibility for what happens.

In short, self-discipline requires taking responsibility for your life, believing that it will be what *you* make it, not what circumstances, or someone else, makes it.

COURAGE

Courage is essential to successful leadership, but not necessarily the kind of courage we usually think of: the courage to face *physical* danger. Much more important is that a leader have the courage to overcome the fear of failure, of being embarrassed, of becoming unpopular or disliked, or of being seen as different. The most important characteristics of this kind of courage are: *commitment*, *sacrifice*, and *unselfishness*.

Commitment

Courage requires the kind of commitment that allows ordinary people to accomplish extraordinary things.

Whether it's called persistence, perseverance, dedication, or fortitude, nothing that's worthwhile is accomplished without it. In fact, the value of anything is determined by how difficult it is to get. That's also why the more difficult the task, the harder it is to find a person who is willing to do it, and stay with it until it's finished.

Most people base their self-expectations on what they *know* they can do. They prefer what's known as a "slam dunk," to the risk of failure. Those who *excel*, on the other hand, do so because they set high expectations for themselves – higher than the most other people. Then they make a commitment to do whatever it takes to reach their goal, despite any obstacles they may encounter. Do they always succeed? Of course not; at least not on the first attempt. But they don't give up; they try, and try again.

It's easy to begin a task, but it takes commitment to perse-
vere in the face of everyday frustrations, disappointments, and
failures, especially when you have high expectations. That's why
so few people take the difficult path, and why those few who do
are so valuable: they can be depended upon to set high expectations for whatever they do, then see every job through to com-
pletion. Committed people are the ones we always count on to
get the job done.

Sacrifice

Life is full of sacrifices. Everything that's worthwhile has a
cost. And because most of us can't do everything we'd like to
do, and can't have everything we'd like to have, we have to
make choices. Every choice is a tradeoff, and every time we
choose one thing, it means giving up something else.

But it isn't as much of a sacrifice when we do something for
our own benefit, as when we do it for someone else. It's easier
when we give up something we'd like to have, in order to get
something we value more; easier because it's for *us*. I said "easier" rather than "easy," because sacrifice is never easy, even
when it is for our own benefit.

For example, one of the most important decisions most people face, at some point in their life, is whether to go to college, or
not. We know that going to college will require major sacrifices
in time, money, effort, and even fun, and the easiest choice may
seem to be to skip college, get a job, and enjoy life. The more
difficult choice would be to commit the next four years to
working and worrying your way to a degree, and spending thousands of dollars in the process – money you may have to work
for years to repay.

Why, then, does anyone ever go to college, when it looks so
much easier and enjoyable to go out and get a job? Those who

do it believe it will pay off in the long run, because they're confident that once they've graduated they'll have a better life, for the *rest* of their life.

Unselfishness

It is one thing to sacrifice to get things for *ourselves*, and something else, again, to sacrifice for the benefit of someone else. But that's what the leaders have to do: sacrifice their own interests to serve the best interests of those they lead. That's what it means to be unselfish: putting your duty before yourself.

And that's the heart of leadership: putting your followers ahead of yourself; doing what's best for *them*. Never forget that, because if your followers ever sense that you put your own interests before theirs, they will have difficulty ever believing in you again.

Discussions of leadership invariably get around to the question of how to lead. Centuries ago, Machiavelli pondered the question, "Should a leader strive to be loved, or to be feared?" For me, the right answer is "neither."

Those who lead by fear rely on the threat of punishment for their power. But the threat of punishment is always demoralizing, and never motivates anyone for very long. So attempting to lead by fear is a disincentive for your followers, and a disservice to your organization.

On the other hand, attempting to be loved is seldom effective, either, because this kind of leader too often tries to avoid making "hard" decisions—those that might be unpopular. Unfortunately, for most of the important decisions that we're inevitably faced with, popular decisions will *not* be the *right* decisions, in the long run.

So every leader should avoid "popularity traps," in which they're tempted to make a decision that will please people, or at least not make them unhappy. But it's seldom possible to make a decision that is both popular and best for the organization, and if you do try to make a decision based on its popularity, you're likely to be mortgaging your organization's future to feed your own ego.

That's why neither trying to be feared or to be loved is likely to make a leader successful. The best strategy is to earn the *respect* of followers, with the knowledge that respect doesn't come from popularity, but from being both firm and fair.

The *right* decisions—those that *should* be made—will *never* be popular with everybody, and *always* unpopular with some people. Nevertheless, neither popularity nor consensus should be considerations in decision-making. Leaders owe it to their constituents to make decisions that will result in the best long-term outcome for their organization. Long-term decisions always require short-term sacrifices, and any decision that requires followers to make sacrifices is likely to be unpopular.

So the best leaders will always be unpopular with some of their followers, and may, at times, be unpopular with *all* of them.

DELEGATION/EMPOWERMENT

Power is the ability to influence the actions of others, and there are positions in every organization that are endowed with authority that gives a person the right to command and judge the individuals who report to him.

While power is an important part of organizational life, the most effective organizations are those in which power is *balanced*. Instead of leaving it in the hands of a few, they share it as widely as possible; they *empower* employees at all levels.

Empowerment

When a leader shares power with those who report to her, she gives them more choice in how they do their jobs. Empowerment includes providing as much information as possible, encouraging and assisting workers in increasing their knowledge and skills, and delegating decision-making authority to those who do the work.

Empowerment is based on the belief that most people, regardless of their level in the organization, are capable of handling more responsibility than they've traditionally been given. All employees should be entrusted with as much authority as they need to become self-sufficient. Give them all the responsibility they can handle, and enough authority to allow them to make as many of their own decisions as possible.

That requires an organizational culture that nurtures people; a culture based on trust and mutual support, and an atmosphere in which employees can discuss ideas, take risks, cooperate, and make their own decisions. That kind of an environment is only possible if it's fully supported by the organization's leaders and by the right organization structure.

Leaders must encourage innovation, which includes tolerating the mistakes and false-starts that are an integral part of experimentation. Leaders must also provide direction, by clarifying the organization's mission and goals, setting high expectations, helping workers set high expectations for themselves, and radiating a level of confidence that will help people build confidence in themselves.

The organization's structure should be as organic (i.e., loosely structured) as possible, in contrast with the more traditional mechanistic structure, with its rigid hierarchy and centralized authority. In this new type of organization, selection of leaders should be based on their willingness to share power, and selection of employees should take into consideration their willingness to take responsibility, and cooperate with others.

In short, empowerment means leaders *delegating* as much power as possible to their followers, and workers taking more responsibility for their own work, and having more authority to make their own decisions.

Delegation

Genuine delegation is when leaders delegate not only the responsibility for doing something, but also the *authority* to make the decisions necessary for getting it done. That involves more risk for leaders, and requires more trust between leaders and followers.

But the willingness to delegate is a major difference between managing people and leading them. It defines how much responsibility we entrust to our followers; how much latitude we give them in determining how to do their jobs; and how much authority we allow them for making their own decisions.

A leader must be confident that delegating power to followers will *not* make her position less secure, nor more vulnerable; only more effective.

STRATEGIC THINKING

An important requirement for a leader, which may be somewhat less necessary for a manager, is the ability to think strategically. Strategic thinking begins with a vision, because without a vision there is no leadership.

A vision is a look into the future, and a plan for leading the organization into that future. It is based on the belief that the organization that creates its own future can *control* what happens to it, rather than waiting to see how the company will be affected by future events. But while vision can provide a glimpse of the organization's desired future, that future will remain only a dream until strategic thinking helps make it a reality.

There are several different perspectives on strategic thinking. One school of thought focuses on getting the most from the organization's current resources. This is a conservative approach: "this is what we have to work with; what can we do with it?" It's based on making do with what the organization currently has to work with. While that approach can be appropriate for some situations, as a primary strategy it is likely to concentrate too much on what *is*, rather than what *could be*, so it isn't likely to do much for the organization's long-term potential.

Another approach, also based getting the most out of *current* resources, is to leverage those resources to the maximum, in a way that gains a competitive advantage, and puts competitors at a disadvantage. While also conservative, because it is constrained by available resources, this approach utilizes those resources more aggressively, to develop a plan that's offensive, rather than passive.

A third form of strategic thinking is based on developing the organization's mission and vision *without* considering current resources. This approach focuses on dreaming big; setting high expectations; focusing on what the organization *might be able* to do; what it potentially *could become*. It is based on the belief that if you want something badly enough, you can find ways to obtain the necessary resources.

While some may view this third approach as a high-risk way of planning, it need not be. Having high expectations and acting responsibly are not mutually exclusive.

Whichever approach is used, the core of strategic thinking is to make your organization *different* from the competition; different in the sense that your competitive strategy satisfies customers' needs in a way that competitors can't match. Whether you do that that with products or services, or by the way they are delivered, doesn't matter as much as how the customers feel about what they get for their money.

SUMMARY

Historically, the success of organizations was usually determined by how well they were managed: how tightly they controlled their processes and their finances. Since they relied heavily on unskilled employees to do their work, managers were essential to monitoring and controlling every step of those processes.

But today's companies are more knowledge-based, and their success depends on the knowledge of the people they hire. Because of their education and training, these employees are hired for more specialized work; work that they *know* how to do, so they don't need managers to *tell them*.

Whereas traditional companies relied heavily on management and managers—to control *how* people did their jobs—today's organizations have a greater need for leadership and leaders, to tell workers *what* to do, but not how. Whereas unskilled workers needed oversight and control, knowledge workers need only direction and goals.

Leaders lead as much by their example—*what* they do, and *who* they are—as by direction, which means they must have clear self-awareness, so they can see themselves as others see them, and know where they need to improve.

Leaders need courage, not to face physical danger, but to overcome the fear of failure, of embarrassment, of unpopularity, or of being seen as different. Most of all they must have the courage to make the *right* decisions, rather than those that are popular, even though they know that such decisions may ultimately be unpopular with many of their followers.

Leaders need confidence, in themselves and in their followers, to enable sharing their power and decision-making authority. And they must be willing to take the blame for anything that goes wrong. That requires trusting people, sometimes with no guarantee that an employee, particularly one who is still untested, will live up to that trust.

Nevertheless, a leader should begin by giving every person the benefit of the doubt, *once*. Those rare people who turn out not to justify that trust shouldn't be trusted in the future, but that shouldn't deter the leader from continuing to be the first to trust. He should do so with confidence that most of the time that trust will be rewarded by the other person's sense of obligation and responsibility. Followers who respect their leader will do anything they can to keep from letting him/her down.

Finally, leaders have to think strategically, look to the future, and make the short-term sacrifices are inevitably necessary to achieve long-term success. Strategic thinking isn't limited to planning; it's also essential to the successful implementation of a plan.

Perhaps the major difference between the most successful companies and their less-successful peers is that their leaders are better strategic thinkers.

16 | COMMUNICATION

"Society evolves this way,
not by shouting each other down,
but by the unique capacity of unique, individual human beings
to comprehend each other."
(Lewis Thomas, 1913-1993)

Communication: "The exchange of thoughts,
messages, or information."
(American Heritage Dictionary, 1983)

Your ability to communicate has a lot to do with your personal effectiveness, whether you're working *with* people, *for* them, or they're working for you. You have to know when to listen and when to speak, and have a genuine desire to understand those with whom you communicate.

Good communication is a lot more than just talking, or sending messages; it's a circular process, that includes *sending*, *receiving*, and *understanding*. Absent any of those three there won't be real communication.

SENDING

Sending simply means giving information to others. Although it is considered the life-blood of an organization, some organizations seem to think information should only be given out "as-needed": if you don't need it to do your job, you shouldn't have it.

Executives usually justify that by concerns about security, confusion, morale, or misinterpretation.

- security—we can't let this get out to our competitors or to the general public;
- confusion—this information (especially financial) will only confuse employees;
- morale—bad news is likely to demoralize workers;
- misinterpretation—people won't understand why we spent money on this (e.g., company airplane, sales meeting in Las Vegas, etc.,) so we'd better keep it confidential; make it available only to those who *need* to know it.

But none of those are valid reasons for withholding information; in fact, the less information an organization provides, the more it undermines people's trust in the organization's leadership, and the more suspicious they become of their leaders' motives. On the other hand, a company can build trust by giving everyone in the organization access to all the information they desire, with the possible exceptions of proprietary information, or information that is legally prohibited.

While we usually think of it as talking, sending can be done in a number of ways, including:

- face-to-face, either one-on-one or in groups;
- telephone conversations;
- media presentations, audio and video;
- hard-copy, by memoranda, letters, or faxes;
- electronically, through email and text-messaging.

Face-to-Face

Face-to-Face communication allows a speaker to express feelings and emotions in ways that can inspire, motivate, and share vibrant images. It can also demonstrate a speaker's genuineness, enthusiasm, excitement, and commitment, through tone of voice and vocal inflections, as well as facial expressions, body language, and gestures.

Face-to-face communication gives speakers the opportunity to "read" how their audiences are responding, and tailor their messages accordingly. And they have the additional advantage of allowing questions, giving listeners the opportunity to satisfy their curiosity, calm their fears, and improve their understanding.

Telephone

A phone conversation also lets listeners ask questions, and hear the speaker's tone of voice and vocal inflections, but doesn't allow the listener to observe facial expressions or body language.

Media

Video presentations can have all of the advantages of face-to-face, except the opportunity for the presenters to "read" their audiences, or answer questions.

Audio-only presentations are similar to video, but without an audience's ability to see the speaker's facial expressions or body language.

Hard-Copy

Letters, memoranda, and faxes are just words on paper, and the printed word lacks the personal touches we get from voice, or body language. Of course, a gifted writer can bring the printed word to life, but most of us aren't that gifted.

But hard-copy does offer one advantage over face-to-face and telephone communication: the opportunity for a writer to carefully think through the intended message and, if necessary, revise it before sending it. That can help avoid the knee-jerk responses that we sometimes make, and later wish we could take back.

Electronic

Email is similar to hard-copy, but has two additional advantages: 1) speed – it is virtually instantaneous; and 2) cost – it is essentially free.

Text messaging has the advantages of email, but a potential disadvantage: the more quickly it's done, and the more it relies on acronyms, the more likely it is to be misunderstood. That reduces its value as a communication tool, except to those who know the sender so intimately they don't have to interpret a message literally; they can read between the lines and understand the sender's intentions.

Regardless of how you send a message, it is important to remember that the more you know about a topic, the greater the risk of your message being misinterpreted or misunderstood. That's called "information asymmetry," which means that one person in a conversation, or a negotiation, has a lot more information than the other party.

So, when you're an expert on a subject, or know a lot more about it than those with whom you are discussing it, be aware that they may not understand what you're trying to say, or may misinterpret it. In that case, it's your responsibility to get enough feedback from them that you'll know when and where to simplify your message, or to provide more information.

Of course, the best way to overcome information asymmetry is getting to know your audience, beforehand. Find out how much they know about your subject, so you can adapt your message to their level of understanding, and make it as specific as necessary to get it across in a way that they understand it.

RECEIVING

The receiver's role in communication is not just listening, and it isn't only for face-to-face discussions, or phone conversations. Receiving also applies to media presentations, as well as hard-copy and electronic transmissions. Serious receivers – those who genuinely *want* to understand what's being communicated—don't just listen; they bring all of their senses into play. They observe, feel, sense, and do whatever else is necessary to accurately interpret what the sender is trying to say.

Effective receiving requires much more than just *being* there; *attention* and *interest* are also essential. In that sense, you won't be an effective receiver when you're thinking about something else, like how you're going to respond when the other party is finished. Listening means giving your full attention to what's being said, or presented, because if you don't listen well you may not *understand* what's being communicated, and *without understanding there is no communication*. And it helps if you can take a genuine interest in what's being discussed; interest is a major aid to understanding.

UNDERSTANDING

Understanding is the real key to effective communication. People who hear or see a discussion or presentation seldom have the same understanding of the message. We see what we see and hear what we hear from the perspective of our own experience, so receivers are likely to have a variety of interpretations, unless there's further clarification.

The best lubricant to understanding is a sincere desire to know what the other person means, but that won't happen if you try to fit the message into the context that's most comfortable for you. You have to make a conscious effort to understand the message from the sender's point of view, or there won't be true communication. Effective receivers have empathy for the sender, and take an interest in what he's trying to say.

Following is a list of the sending methods we've just discussed, in order of their effectiveness—the accuracy with which a message is likely to be interpreted:

1. Face-to-face communication between two people.
2. Face-to-face communication among a group of people.
3. Telephone conversation between two people.
4. Tele-conference.
5. Media presentation – video and audio.
6. Media presentation – audio only.
7. Hard-copy—memorandum, letter, fax.
8. Electronic—email
9. Electronic—text messaging.

As previously mentioned, face-to-face is usually the most effective way of communicating, because participants can hear tone of voice, observe facial expressions and body language, and ask questions for clarification. Email and text messaging are the least effective, because tone of voice, facial expressions, and body language are not available. In fact, it's been suggested that, due to the high risk of misinterpreting the printed word, email should be used only to communicate non-emotional information.

And consider this: in a discussion about face-to-face conversation, Wellner suggests that 55 percent of the meaning of a conversation is transmitted by facial expression and body language, and 38 percent through voice inflection. That means only 7 percent of the intent of a message is transmitted by words alone. (2005:37-38)

That should be a warning that when we communicate through email, text messages, memos, letters, or faxes, more than 90 percent of our meaning can be lost in translation, which can leave a huge gap in a receiver's ability to understand the message.

Phone conversations are somewhat better, capturing both the words (7 percent) and voice inflection (38 percent), but that still leaves 55 percent of the meaning at risk of being misinterpreted.

It should be obvious, then, that face-to-face communication has the best chance of being clearly understood. With that in mind, we should seriously consider limiting hard-copy and electronic messages to *factual* information; never anything that's emotional or that might be misinterpreted.

Yet there is a positive side to hard-copy communication. In face-to-face discussions and phone conversations, we sometimes respond, on the spur of the moment, with comments that we haven't had time to think through completely. The obligation we sometimes feel to "carry" our part of the conversation may pressure us into responding before we've had time to really think about it, and the more urgent, or spontaneous, the discussion, the more that risk increases.

When that's the case, it may be wise to delay answering until we've had time to digest the information, then respond in writing. Here, written communication is likely to be more effective because we can take time to think about the situation, write our response, and revise it until we feel comfortable, before sending it. That's particularly true when a conversation becomes more emotional than objective. Then, a written response gives us an opportunity to express *our* feelings, and time to cool down before we decide whether or not to send it.

At one point in my business career, I became so frustrated with a situation in my company that I decided to write a letter of concern to the CEO. After I had re-written it several times, to a point where I felt it stated my concerns effectively, if not eloquently, I decided to share it with my boss before sending it on. After looking it over, he brought it back to me, with just one comment: "This will be one of the finest letters that you *didn't* send." He didn't have to say anything else; his message was loud and clear: "Don't let your emotions overrule your objectivity." (I later decided not to send the letter, and was thankful I hadn't.)

QUESTIONS

Questions are a valuable part of understanding. Their most obvious use is by receivers, to help them understand the sender's intentions. Some examples of that kind of *active- listening* question:

- "This is what I heard you say.........Is it accurate?"
- "Could you repeat that?"
- "Does that mean....?"

But questions can also be used by *senders,* to get more information from receivers—comments, opinions, ideas—and to help clarify the sender's intentions.

"Asking good questions, rather than giving answers, forces you to listen attentively to your constituents and what they are saying. This action demonstrates your respect for their ideas and opinions." (Kouzes and Posner, 2007:84)

"Asking what others think facilitates participation in whatever decision will ultimately be determined and consequently increases support for that decision." (Ibid.)

"In the old organization we asked 'who' questions: Who is accountable? Who screwed this up? In the new organization we ask 'why' or 'how' questions: Why has this problem occurred? How can we improve the system and eliminate the cause of this problem? The old managers gave orders or advice and exercised control. The new managers ask questions and promote communication, knowledge, and understanding." (Scholtes, 1998:263)

Scholtes offers seven "All-Purpose Questions" (Ibid:266-269) here paraphrased:

1. Why?
   When a problem occurs, ask why it occurred (not who was responsible.) Ask "Why?" as many times as it takes to get to the root cause of the problem.

2. What's the purpose?
   When someone proposes something new, ask what is its purpose? What are his intentions?

3. What will it take to accomplish it?
   How will it be done? By what method?

4. How will it affect our customers?
   How do you know that?

5. Why do you believe that?
   What are your assumptions?

6. What information do you have?
   What data might you get? How do you know?.

7. Where did you get your information?
   How do you know it's valid?

UPWARD COMMUNICATION

It isn't uncommon for organizational protocol to demand that all *upward* communication go through the chain of command. That means if you want to communicate with someone *above* your boss, you should first ask your boss, so he/she isn't left out of the communication loop.

The intentions of this practice are: to promote respect for the chain of command—an issue of authority; and to emphasize employees' responsibility to their supervisors—an issue of loyalty. And that's an important consideration: each of us should be loyal to the person to whom we report.

And, ideally, all of those bosses—executives, managers, supervisors—will be open-minded, and responsive to questions, concerns, and suggestions from their subordinates. But, unfortunately, there are bosses who are not that receptive, which can put their subordinates in a difficult situation: "What can we do when the boss only communicates in one direction; when he won't listen?" "What can we do when we disagree with him, his decisions, or the way he treats us?"

In that situation you have three choices: 1) discuss it directly with the boss—tell him how you feel; 2) just put up with it—grin and bear it; or 3) quit, or transfer out.

Option 1—discuss it

The best option is to work it out person to person, and that works well when the boss is open to questions, comments, and suggestions. But a manager who doesn't like being questioned or challenged, is likely to resent it, and may hold it against you. That doesn't mean you shouldn't discuss it with him, especially before choosing one of the other options.

Those bosses may be that way because they think they're smarter than their workers, or they may be so insecure they're afraid being questioned by their workers will undermine their authority. Whatever the reason, they can be frustrating to work for, and if your boss is one of them, you may have to consider option 2) put up with him, or 3) quit, or transfer out.

Option 2—put up with it

For some people—particularly those who are content doing what they're told without questioning the boss—this can be a good option. In fact, for people who have an external locus of control (see Chapter 15) this may be the best of the three choices.

But those who want to know *why* things are done the way they're done, or who have ideas for better ways of doing things, won't be content to put up with a non-receptive boss. For them, that may be the worst choice, one they'll pay for in frustration, poor morale, and loss of self-esteem. So this option will only be acceptable as a short-term solution; until they can find a job in another department or another company (option 3.)

Option 3—quit, or transfer out

This, of course, is the last choice, but may turn out for the best, in the long-run. In any case, it's best not to exercise this option until you have another job lined up; until then, stick with option 2.

But there is another possibility, although a politically-risky one. That's to bypass your boss and go directly to *his* boss. It's risky in two ways: your boss will almost certainly resent your going around him, and his boss is likely to resent the fact that you've violated the chain of command.

The first question he'll ask is have you discussed it with your boss. I you haven't, he'll insist that you do so before he can meet with you. Even if he hears you out, he's likely to support your boss, in which case you will probably have lost stature with both of them, which may have an affect on your future with the company.

The best possible outcome, and it's a long shot, is if you've been able to make such a strong case against your boss that his boss agrees with you. But that's not likely unless your boss's actions have been so blatant that your concerns will be strongly supported by your co-workers.

Communicating with a boss who is open and receptive can be very reassuring to workers, but one who is close-minded, defensive, or difficult, can be seriously demoralizing. In fact, research has found that bad bosses are the most common reason for employees quitting their jobs.

SUMMARY

Good communication is much more than just speaking or presenting. They are just part of the first step in a three-part process: *sending*, *receiving*, and *understanding*. Communication is a circular process that begins with sending, followed by receiving, then understanding, and back to sending.

Communication begins when one person wants to say something to someone else; one person or many. The message can be sent in many ways, but how well it will be understood depends on the method.

Regardless of how a message is sent, communication depends on a *receiver*—someone to hear, see, or read it. But even having a receiver doesn't guarantee effective communication; the receiver must *understand* what the sender is trying to say.

Understanding is the key to successful communication, and it depends on two things: how effectively the sender transmits her intentions; and how well the receiver interprets the sender's true meaning. The clearest understanding occurs with receivers who genuinely want to know the sender's intentions, and can ask *questions* to help that understanding.

Questions can help in two ways: when used by a receiver to clarify the message; and when used by a sender, to learn how effectively the message is being received, or to more actively involve the receivers in the conversation.

The ability to communicate well is a critical component in our effectiveness, both as individuals and in organizations. And a clear understanding of the advantages and disadvantages of all the methods of communication that are available to us is an important part of effective communication.

A final caution about electronic communication: recent studies suggest that people are significantly more likely to *lie* when communicating by email. A researcher found "...emails don't give you non-verbal and behavioral clues, like fidgety body language or shifty eyes,... That leaves a lot of room for misinterpretation and, ... deception." (Fisher, 2008:57)

17 | THE ORGANIZATION'S ATMOSPHERE[1]

"It is the test of an organization to make ordinary human beings
perform better than they seem capable of,
to bring out whatever strength there is in its members,
and to use each man's strength to help all the others perform."
(Peter Drucker, 1909-2005)

A fellow professor used to begin every management class with a reminder that one of the primary responsibilities of a manager is to "create the atmosphere," by which he meant develop and maintain the kind of organizational environment that will nurture and inspire employees.

Have you ever walked into an organization where you could actually *feel* the atmosphere? I have, but not often; only in those rare companies that understand how important its atmosphere is. How does one "feel" a company's atmosphere?

Through the attitudes of its employees: how they talk, how they walk, and how optimistic they are. Let me tell you about one such company.

I was invited for visit and plant tour of a small manufacturing company, to learn more about its incentive program. When I walked into the lobby I was

---

[1]Portions of this chapter have been excerpted from *Managing Strategically for Superior Performance,* 3rd Edition (O'Neal, 2008, Chapter 9), and from *Developing Leaders* (O'Neal, 2009, Chapter 13)

greeted by a friendly receptionist (no surprise there; we expect receptionists to be welcoming, don't we?) who asked me to have a seat while she located my tour guide.

While I waited, every employee who happened to pass through the lobby greeted me with a smile and a sincere "good morning," "how are you?" or "welcome to _____." Yet every one of them seemed to be in a hurry; none were just *strolling* through, as you see in many organizations; they all walked with a sense of urgency.

While I was touring the factory, I was treated with the same kind of friendliness by everyone I met; the kind that makes you feel welcome. And I saw, everywhere, the same "hustle" I had witnessed in the lobby. Seldom have I ever felt so welcome and so comfortable in a company, especially in one with that sense of urgency.

The employees' pride in their organization was palpable, and they appeared to genuinely enjoy working there, and had great respect for their fellow employees. It was obvious that they saw themselves as a tightly-knit team that depended on each member for its overall success, not as just a group of individuals who happened to be working for the same company.

I had visited that company to learn how its incentive plan worked, and came away impressed with how effective it had been in creating a cooperative, enthusiastic, high-performing culture.

CULTURE

For years, business theorists have debated which of a company's constituents are most important; is it customers, employees, or owners/investors?

Salespeople argue that without customers there would be no revenue from which to pay employees, or to reward investors. Human resource people insist that, without the capabilities and efforts of its employees, the organization would *have* no customers. And finance people claim that without investors' money there would be no company, in the first place.

Of course all three views are right—investors, customers and employees are absolutely essential to the organization. That's why it's difficult to accept the argument that any one is more important than the others.

But what if, rather than debating which is most important, we considered it from a chicken-and-egg perspective: which comes first?

We could make a case that first we need investors; otherwise there'll be no money to hire employees or to produce products or services. But investors aren't likely to risk their money unless they are confident the company will be successful; and who will make it successful? Satisfied customers. But then, who will satisfy those customers? Employees, of course.

So, investors won't invest unless they have confidence in employees' ability to satisfy customers. Without investors there'll be no employees; and without employees there'll be no products or services to satisfy customers. From that perspective—the one I've used throughout this book—employees should be first among an organization's stakeholders.

Jim Collins, author of *Good to Great,* one of the most successful business books ever written, puts it this way "If we can get the right people on the bus, ...and the wrong people off the bus, then we'll figure out how to take it someplace great." (2001:41)

Employees may not be more important than customers or investors, but they should be first priority, because they have to be in place before the company can attract either investors or customers. Here's the way it works: employees plan and produce products and services that will attract and satisfy customers, and the revenue from those customers provides the return on investment that satisfies investors.

Culture is defined as "The arts, beliefs, customs, institutions, and all other products of human work and thought created by a people or group at a particular time." (American Heritage Dictionary, 1983.)

Although that definition is precise and specific, for our purposes culture can be defined more simply, as a set of shared values that influences behavior within the organization. That's similar to "The way we do things around here." (Bower, 1996:41), and "What people do when no one is telling them what to do." (Colvin,1997:300).

No matter how we define it, culture can have a powerful influence on the decisions and actions of an organization. Employees and their actions *are* the culture, which plays a major role in defining what the organization *is* and how it does what it does.

An organization's culture is usually developed in one of two ways: the firm can deliberately develop a specific kind of culture, or it can do nothing, and let the culture develop on its own.

When an organization doesn't develop its own culture, it may be because management doesn't feel culture is important, or doesn't realize how much culture can influence its success, or failure. Whatever the reason, if the organization doesn't make an effort to develop a culture, one will evolve on its own, probably following the path of least resistance; whichever direction is easiest, or most popular.

But when a culture develops on its own, and doesn't have strong guiding principles, those who make decisions will be more likely to take the easy way (i.e., "go with the flow"), rather than the "right" way. Unfortunately, making the "right" (i.e., morally right) decisions is often more difficult so, in a "default" culture (i.e., one that developed on its own) managers will be less likely to make the hard decisions; and much more likely to take the easy way out.

For example, in some countries paying bribes to influence public officials or customers is an accepted, even expected, practice. While it is illegal for members of U.S.-based firms to engage in such activities, in any country, the unwritten, but clearly understood, philosophy of many of them is "we'll do whatever we have to (i.e., do what everyone else does) or be at a competitive disadvantage."

Perhaps it's because that's quicker and easier than trying to develop a competitive advantage based on better products or services. Whatever the reason, that kind of philosophy is much more likely to prevail in a weak, or undefined, culture than in one that has been deliberately developed and nurtured.

Every company owes its employees a strong culture; one based on social responsibility, that encourages them to always do what's right.

SOCIAL RESPONSIBILITY

Every organization should make sure its decisions and actions are guided by a sense of social responsibility, defined as the responsibility an organization (including its leaders and members) has to anyone who will be affected by its decisions and actions.

This includes a responsibility to all the organization's stakeholders, to ensure that the decisions and actions of the organization are guided by *moral* principles and actions; *not* by convenience, opportunism, or self-interest.

It should go without saying that all of us, as individuals, have responsibilities to those affected by our decisions and actions. Those are our *ethics*, defined as "... rules or standards governing the conduct of...members..." (The American Heritage Dictionary, 1983).

The cornerstones of individual ethics and organizational social responsibility are the same: a responsibility to recognize and respect the rights of others, and be accountable for our own actions. It sounds so simple and it is, in principle, but not so easy in practice. Why? Because it's sometimes difficult to live up to our values.

VALUES

One of the central concepts of culture is "shared values." A value can be defined "A principle, standard, or quality considered inherently worthwhile or desirable." (American Heritage Dictionary, 1983), or "...an enduring belief that a specific mode of conduct ... is preferable to an opposite... mode of conduct ...." (Rokeach, 1973:5)

Our behavior is influenced by our values. Some of us have values that strongly influence our decisions and actions, while others may be influenced more by circumstances than by any values of their own.

Those with strong values have a clear sense of who they are, what they believe in, and where they're going. Those without a clear sense of their values tend to be influenced by the philosophies of other people; philosophies like "if it feels good, do it". Stated another way, those with strong values have internal direction, while those without them are likely to be influenced more by external factors.

If this sounds similar to *locus of control*, it is. People who feel they can influence outcomes by their own efforts have an *internal* locus of control, while those who think outcomes are beyond their control have an *external* locus of control.

There are both types of people in every organization, and if the organization doesn't try to develop a specific culture, the one that evolves will be driven by those people who have the strongest values, the most powerful drive to achieve their own goals, are strongest-willed, or simply the most vocal.

In that type of culture, the values of those with the strongest convictions are likely to become the organization's "shared values," and people who don't have strong values are likely to simply follow them. Unfortunately, the culture that results is likely to use the organization's resources to achieve its own objectives, which may not be in the best interests of the organization as a whole.

The organization that decides to develop its own culture will begin by clearly defining its guiding values. Those values will then become the values that will be shared by all organizational members, and the principles that govern behavior throughout the organization.

The organization's culture should be reinforced by its incentive plan, which should be designed to reward people who support the organization's values and culture. The incentives, along with the organizational value system, will help guide the behavior of those employees who do not have a strong sense of their own values. That way, they will be less likely to be influenced by peer pressure, or by values, decisions, or actions that are not consistent with those of the organization.

On the other hand, employees who *do* have strong values will have to come to terms with the organization's values. If some of the organization's values are in conflict with their own, they will have to decide if they can live within the organizational value system while at work. If not, they may have to leave the organization.

In any case, a strong set of organizational values sends the message "here's the behavior we expect of everyone, and if you can't or won't play according to these rules, there's no place for you in this culture."

Values give *meaning* to what we do; they influence our individual attitudes and behavior, and play an important role in organizational strategy. Values, along with history and experience, define an organization's culture which, in turn, generates a commitment among the organization's members to beliefs and values that are larger than their own. Culture influences how employees operate: how they process information, make decisions, and interpret and manage the organization's external environment.

Developing the right culture takes a concentrated effort, and maintaining it requires a long-term commitment. Nurturing a culture requires an employee-selection process that ensures that new employees not only have the skills and capabilities that are needed, but also personal values that are not in conflict with the organization's values. Once new employees have been selected, it's essential to gain their commitment to the organization, its mission, and its goals.

Proper selection helps ensure that everyone in the organization will share and actively support its values.

EMPLOYEE SATISFACTION

Research has found direct relationships between personal satisfaction, self-motivation, and individual performance. Furthermore, it has shown a significant, measurable, correlation between employee satisfaction and customer satisfaction, and between customer satisfaction and organizational revenue. Those relationships suggest that satisfying employees is not only the key to motivation, but also to organizational success. What are the keys to employee satisfaction?

Griffin discusses two dimensions of satisfaction: *motivation*, and *hygiene*. (2008:295)

His motivation factors include: achievement, recognition, responsibility, advancement and growth, and the work itself. You'll notice how similar they are to the needs Maslow identified.

Griffin's hygiene factors are: supervisors, working conditions, interpersonal relations, pay and security, and company policies and administration.

Another way of looking at Griffin's dimensions is: motivation factors are *satisfiers*, and hygiene factors are *dissatisfiers*. Money, for example, has been long recognized as a *dis*satisfier, because it seldom makes anyone happy for long—a few weeks, at most—after which it is more likely to become a dissatisfier.

With that in mind, an organization should pay particular attention to the hygiene factors (e.g., paying competitive wages, instead of trying to low-ball salaries, or trying to buy satisfaction with excessive wages.) Then it should focus on the *satisfiers,* which usually don't cost much, if anything at all, except in the time it takes to maintain good personal relations. But the payoffs can be huge. As employee satisfaction increases turnover will inevitably decrease, reducing recruiting and training costs, which can be considerable.

Employee satisfaction is based primarily on how well a person *likes* his work; enjoys what he does. A number of factors affect job satisfaction, but perhaps most important are: doing a job that's important and interesting; a job that's challenging, and in which he spends most of his time doing things that fully utilize his education, training, experience, and expertise.

Working on things that are not important, work that isn't challenging, and feeling under-utilized, are three of the most powerful demoralizers. All of those can be corrected by utilizing every person to the fullest extent of his capabilities, not just part of the time, but all of the time.

SUMMARY

An organization's internal atmosphere can have a major influence on its success or failure. If the organization doesn't develop a particular culture, one *will* evolves on its own. But a culture that evolves on its own is not as likely to be an asset to the organization as one that has been consciously developed. In fact, a self-developed culture is more likely to be a liability than an asset.

Its culture should be based on the set of values the organization feels will best guide the kind of behavior it wants from its people. When developed this way, the culture can powerfully influence desirable behavior, and be a strong deterrent to improper or unacceptable behavior. Culture influences employee attitudes, and constantly reminds them of the organization's values, beliefs and responsibilities.

Positive cultures are built on values like honesty, integrity, loyalty and trust. Organizations can nurture and maintain that kind of culture through their hiring practices, reward and incentive programs, day-to-day communication, and orientation and training. But perhaps the most powerful influence on an organization's culture is the example set by members of the top management team. What they *do* and *how* they do it send a much clearer message of their values and beliefs than anything they could possibly *say*.

An organization's culture and values are part of its legacy, and the stronger they are, the longer the organization will live. And organizational longevity can only be ensured if the organization's culture, along with its history, are valued enough by the current generation of employees that they will feel that it's important to hand them over to the next generation.

That's why it is so important that every employee and every manager, regardless of their ages, be tolerant, patient, and understanding of generation-gap differences in how we view the world and the way those who are much younger, or much older, may see it. We should respect their perspectives, even though they may be considerably different than ours.

As organizations become more dependent on knowledge and less on manual labor, the people they hire will expect more flexibility in how, where, and when they do their jobs. That means they will not be easily monitored or controlled. These organizations will need to be much more "organic," in the sense that their *outcomes* will be predictable, even though the processes through which they are achieved may not be.

When we can't *directly* control people, or what they do, we have to depend on other ways of making sure they don't go beyond certain boundaries. A strong culture provides well-defined boundaries for even the most chaotic processes. And there are no better boundaries than the values, beliefs, and understood practices of a strong culture.

A final note on organizational atmosphere, as discussed in Chapter 13: whenever something goes wrong, as it inevitably will, we should never look for *who* is to blame; search, instead, for *what* is to blame: the *cause* of the problem. We should always assume that good people don't make mistakes *deliberately*, and they will seldom make the same mistake twice. So we should give them the benefit of the doubt, by always looking for solutions, not culprits.

<table>
<tr><td>18</td><td># THE EXTERNAL ENVIRONMENT[1]</td></tr>
</table>

"You see things; and you say, "why?"
but I dream things that never were;
and I say, "why not?"
(George Bernard Shaw, 1856-1950)

Some organizations seem to operate as though they are closed, self-contained systems; that they have complete control over everything they do and anything that might affect them. But in reality all organizations are open systems; they operate in, and are affected by external environments they can't control. Figure 8 illustrates the relationship between an organization and its external environment.

INPUTS ⟶ PRODUCTION ⟶ OUTPUTS

Figure 8. The Organization

The box labeled "Production" represents the internal part of the organization; everything that takes place inside it; the processes it can actually control.

---

[1]Portions of this chapter have been excerpted from *Managing Strategically for Superior Performance,* 3rd Edition (O'Neal, 2008, Chapter 6)

The "Inputs" arrow depicts resources that are essential to the organization, but have to come from the outside; from the external environment. Those inputs can be grouped into two categories: labor (people) and capital (money.) Capital is used to purchase the raw materials, equipment, information, and physical facilities the company needs for the production process; to produce its products or services.

The "Outputs" arrow represents those products or services. Production, itself, is an internal process, but once inputs have been converted into outputs, the external environment is essential as a market for the outputs. It is customers, people from outside the organization, who will purchase those outputs.

Because of its continual need to obtain inputs and sell outputs, every organization is dependent on its external environment. That's why an organization's success is never completely within its own control; success depends on how well the organization is able to respond to the uncertainty of the external environment. But before it can respond to the external environment, the organization must understand it, and how it might be affected by it.

Whereas we can control what happens inside the organization, at first glance the external environment appears to be pretty much beyond our control. But that doesn't mean it's totally unpredictable. As a matter of fact, if we know what to look for we can anticipate many things that are likely happen in the external environment, *before* they happen.

For example, if I throw you a ball, and you see it coming, you will automatically "predict" what you'll need to do to catch it or to avoid being hit by it. At first you may not know exactly where it's heading, but as you watch its progress you will automatically narrow the possible target area.

We do this all the time, much of it almost unconsciously. When we're driving, we often predict whether or not we will have time to pass the car in front of us without colliding with an oncoming car. Almost without thinking about it, we automatically calculate how fast we and other driver are traveling.

In this way, using a combination of experience, perception, attention, and reaction-time, we are able to do a certain amount of predicting. We do it by observing *trends* and *events;* by watching what *has* happened and what *is* happening, then estimating what *will probably* happen.

That requires constantly looking for trends in the external environment, then predicting which are most likely to affect our organization, and how. Once we've become experienced at spotting trends, we'll be able to evaluate, well in advance, which trends are likely to offer opportunities and which may be threats.

OPPORTUNITIES AND THREATS

A *threat* is anything that's potentially *dangerous:* something bad that might happen to us. An *opportunity* is something that seems *favorable*; a possible advantage. Although their definitions are different, both threats and opportunities come from the same sources, usually major trends and events in areas like:

- demographics
- the economy
- education
- technology
- the workplace
- the physical environment
- health care
- globalization
- government/legislation/politics

If we see trends early enough, we can find opportunities where others see only threats. It's all about perception: whether we view something as a threat or an opportunity depends on how we look at it. What one person or organization sees as a threat, someone else will see as an opportunity.

Much of the difference in how we view it is *preparation.* If we've spotted the trend in advance, anticipated how it is likely to affect us, and prepared accordingly, we're likely to be looking forward to the opportunities it offers. But what looks like an opportunity to the prepared organization is more likely to be threatening to someone who is caught off guard. Why is it that some organizations seem well prepared for the future, while others find themselves at the mercy of circumstances?

The difference is usually how strategically they are managed. Those led by strategic thinkers continually monitor their external environments so they can see trends as they develop, then use those insights to prepare for the future. They *manage* how the external environment will affect them.

Others organizations let themselves become so bogged down in *reacting* to the everyday things that happen to them, that they never take the time to look ahead. As a result, they wind up being *captives* of the external environment, and they're the ones in which it isn't unusual to hear busy executives say "We don't have time to plan; we're too busy."

The keys to managing the external environment rather than being managed by it, are *believing* that you can do something about it, then knowing *what* to do, and *how* to do it.

MANAGING THE EXTERNAL ENVIRONMENT

There are a number of strategies that can help an organization reduce the effects of the external environment

Boundary Spanning

Boundary spanning is the first, and most important, step in managing the external environment. It can keep us aware of anything that's happening in the external environment that may affect our organization. Who should be responsible for boundary spanning?

Almost anyone can do it, but some of the best boundary spanners are people whose jobs put them in contact with the outside world. People in sales, service, purchasing, public relations, and human resources, for example, are ideal. In the normal course of their work, they have access to information from suppliers, customers, the community, the industry, and current and potential employees.

They can collect information and observations that will help keep the organization up to date on what *is* happening, able to anticipate what is *likely* to happen, and when, and allow planning accordingly. Boundary spanning is an organization's window on the world, providing information that will help spot future trends while they can still be opportunities; *before* they become threats.

Networking

It's important not to overlook the potential of individual networking as a means of communicating across organizational boundaries. While it's obviously a form of boundary spanning, networking is unique in its more individual, and sometimes personal relationships among people in different organizations.

Networking can have far-reaching effects, particularly when you consider the fact that some of the strongest and most binding relationships between one company and another are really not between the organizations, themselves, but between two individuals.

Buffering

Buffering reduces uncertainty by preventing shortages of inputs and outputs.

The organization's ability to acquire the inputs it needs, when it needs them, can be bolstered by building up inventories of raw materials, equipment, and people, ahead of time. Its ability to make *outputs* available when customers need them can be ensured by increasing inventories of finished goods.

Other ways of buffering are maintaining multiple suppliers (to ensure that critical inputs are always available, regardless of what happens to any single supplier), preventive maintenance (to ensure that work flow isn't interrupted by equipment failures), and recruiting and training employees (to make sure their skills are available *before* they're needed.)

Rationing

Rationing becomes necessary when a company isn't able to supply enough outputs to keep up with demand, so many organizations make rationing an integral part of their competitive strategies.

For example, while organizations that produce *products* can meet increased demand by producing more products or building up inventory, *service* organizations can't do that, because services can't usually be inventoried. Although a service company could increase its capacity, by hiring more people, that increases the risk of laying people off when business slows, which can be a particular problem when demand for a company's output is cyclical.

That's why many service organizations *ration* their services. Restaurants, for example, have a limited number of seats, so getting in during busy times may require reservations in advance. Popular colleges and universities can only accommodate a certain number of students, so they use some kind of priority or standards-based admission system to ration admissions.

Smoothing

Smoothing means leveling the demand for a product or service, and is used when demand varies significantly from hour to hour or day to day. To encourage customers to shift their calls from the busiest times to slower periods, phone companies charge their highest prices for calls made during business hours, and lower prices for evening and weekend calls.

Electric utility companies use a process called "demand metering" to charge customers based on their *highest* demand for electricity, even though that demand may last for only a few minutes at a time. Since electricity is generated at the same time it's being used, it can't be stored, or inventoried. As a result, electric companies have to generate enough electricity to satisfy the highest demand, *all the time*, so it will be available whenever customers need it, even though they may only use it for short periods.

Because they can't be sure how many people will attend each game, sports teams sell season tickets at reduced rates. That guarantees a certain level of income, and smooths out their revenue stream. Magazines and newspapers do the same thing, selling subscriptions to provide a more predictable flow of income than newsstand sales would allow. Auto rental agencies are another example, offering lower rates on weekends, when their cars would usually be idle and bringing in no revenue at all.

Advertising

Companies advertise to build brand loyalty, because they know it increases their customers' switching costs. The more loyal customers are to one brand, the more difficult it is for them to switch to a competitive brand. So brand loyalty makes the demand for a product more consistent; less variable.

Advertising not only helps convince potential customers to try a certain brand, it also reinforces their confidence that they purchased the right product. And the more a company can lock in repeat business, the more it reduces the uncertainty of its revenue stream.

Convincing customers that a product or service is superior in some way—quality, service, features, image with peers, etc.—will make them more likely to continue buying that brand, less inclined to switch to competitive brands, and they may be willing to pay a premium price, as well.

Contracting (Supply Smoothing)

Reaching agreements with major customers, in which the customer commits to purchase specified quantities of products/services over a specified time (e.g., 5000 units over the next 3 years), in exchange for guaranteed prices over that period, benefits both parties.

The seller is guaranteed a certain volume of business in exchange for not raising prices during the term of the contract, and the buyer benefits from stable prices during that period. Although this is an example of the output side of the business, contracts can also be negotiated for inputs, to guarantee the ability to purchase raw material at pre-determined prices.

Co-opting

A popular way of co-opting is through appointments to an organization's board of directors. For example, it isn't unusual for a company to offer a board seat to an executive from its lending institution. The same holds true for retired members of governmental agencies (e.g., the Environmental Protection

Agency); or for retired military officers (by defense contractors). The principal idea of co-opting is to get people into the organization who know how to blunt or buffer issues that offer particular threats to the company, or who can assist in taking advantage of opportunities in their areas of expertise and experience.

Lobbying

Another form of co-opting is hiring lobbyists to influence the passage of legislation that is favorable to the organization, or to fight against legislation that may threaten it. For small organizations, this is often done through trade associations, whose lobbyists work on issues that are of vital interest to all members of the association. Lobbying also results in licensing requirements and regulations that reduce competition in an industry, by making it difficult for new companies to enter an industry.

Strategic Alliances

Another way of reducing the uncertainty of the external environment is for two or more organizations to enter into a strategic alliance. This is usually done with the intention of developing synergies, improving economies of scale, increasing the ability to influence the environment, gaining entry into new markets, or simply eliminating other companies as competitors.

Strategic alliances include acquisitions, in which one firm purchases another; mergers, in which organizations permanently join forces; and joint ventures, in which they enter into temporary cooperative arrangements.

Ultimately, an organization's long-term success depends on how well it is able to anticipate and act on trends and events in the external environment. Those with the clearest windows on the world will be in the best position to develop competitive strategies that can turn potential threats into opportunities. And they will be better able to operate proactively, instead of wasting time and energy reacting to situations they didn't anticipate.

SUMMARY

No matter how effectively an organization operates internally, its success will ultimately be affected by how well it responds to the external environment. Although we cannot control the external environment, there are a number of ways in which we can influence it, or adapt to it.

Most organizations pay close attention to their *competitive* environments, but they often ignore, or give only minimal attention to the part of the external environment that's *outside* of the industry. It's a much broader area, and one from which major trends and events evolve that can affect the organization in the future, with either threats or opportunities. So it's just as important to monitor the *entire* external environment, as it is the competitive arena.

Although we may not be able to predict the future, we can spot trends, sometimes years in advance, that are likely to affect us. Always remember the many businesses that have been devastated by changing technologies (e.g., steam engine, telegraph, telephone, railroads, automobile, airplane), despite the fact that the vast majority of those innovations were under development, and visible, for years before they began to significantly affect organizations.

The best way to manage the external environment is to see those trends as they develop, determine which might offer future opportunities, or threats, for the organization, and prepare accordingly.

19 | MOVING INTO THE FUTURE[1]

"There is nothing more difficult to carry out,
nor more doubtful of success,
nor more dangerous to handle,
than to initiate a new order of things."
(Niccolo Machiavelli, 1469-1527)

The world around us is constantly changing, in ways that affect the way we live and how we do business. When faced with change, our choice is clear: we can resist it, or embrace it.

CHANGE

Among the major forces driving change are:

- global competition,
- new technology,
- government regulation/politics,
- changing consumers and consumer demands,
- demographic shifts,
- environmental activism,
- workplace changes,
- increasing education levels.

---

[1]Portions of this chapter have been excerpted from *Developing Leaders* (O'Neal, 2009, Chapter 15)

One of the best ways to deal with change is to develop an organizational culture that embraces change, makes change a way of life; a culture that changes, not because it has to, but because its members realize that how they respond to change will be a key to their company's future.

Most of us are likely to resist change, at least at first. We resist it because change brings uncertainty, and we much prefer what's familiar over the unknown. We get used to being in our own "comfortable rut," and that's where we prefer to stay, as long as it doesn't get too uncomfortable. It's just easier to keep doing what we've been doing than it is to make the effort to switch to something different. And, since they are staffed by people, it shouldn't come as any surprise that organizations are also more likely to oppose change than to embrace it.

But resisting change isn't necessarily bad. It can provide stability, by making it less likely an organization will be bounced around by a turbulent environment, or by fads, uncertainty, or indecisive decision-making. Although this kind of organization *can* be influenced to change, it's usually only through a deliberate, well-thought-out process, instead of quickly responding to *every* call for change, no matter how arbitrary it may be.

On the other hand, change resistance can be bad if it becomes too deeply embedded in an organization's culture. When that happens, it's likely to resist change so strongly that it becomes a pawn of its external environment and the uncertainties it presents. Then, instead of controlling its own destiny, the organization lets its future be determined by fate—by unplanned change—sometimes with disastrous consequences.

Unplanned change can be forced on an organization, either by an external crisis that puts it at risk, or by a powerful internal coalition trying to serve its own interests. *Planned* change, in contrast, is driven by strategic planning, and begins well before it is needed.

Studies have shown that more than half of startup organizations fail within 5 years of their founding, and only 1 out of every 10 survives for more than 20 years. Failure to change, and to see the need for change are surely major contributors to that mortality rate.

Although any organization is likely to face a crisis at some point, those that have a plan for the future are more likely to anticipate the crisis, and act *before* it reaches a critical point. Those without plans are more likely to delay acting until the situation becomes critical, then be forced to *react* to what's happening to them.

Every organization has a choice: take the initiative, and *lead* change, or resist until the situation is beyond your ability to control it.

LEADING CHANGE

An organization's effectiveness is strongly influenced by how dynamic it is in changing, developing, and improving. In a turbulent industry, an organization must be dynamic, just to keep up, and the most successful organizations are those that develop cultures that *lead* change rather than resist it. Wal-Mart is a good example. Its founder, Sam Walton, deliberately developed an organization culture that would welcome change, and he constantly reinforced that culture by encouraging employees to suggest new ideas for improving the company. That's now become common practice in many organizations, which tap into the creativity of their employees by encouraging them to participate in programs like continuous improvement, quality circles, and six sigma.

The way employees feel about change is affected not only by how clearly they understand *why* changing is important, but also what advantages the change will have for the organization, and for them, personally. Understanding the need for change is essential to developing a culture that will embrace and facilitate change; an understanding that requires employees to know the answers to five questions:

1. W*hat* must change?
2. *Why* is the change necessary? *What* is driving it?
3. W*ho* is driving the change?
4. *How* will it be done?
5. *When* does it have to be done?

Why is the change necessary? Although there are many possibilities, some of the more common drivers of organizational change are changes in:

*   *strategy*—a new strategic plan often requires changes in the organization's structure, and in how resources are allocated;
*   *size* – organizational growth frequently necessitates changing the organization's structure;
*   *technology*—introduction of new technology can change how we do things, and the skills and capabilities they require;
*   *environment*—changes in the environment that are driven by the economy, new competitors, demographic changes, strategic alliances, new legislation, etc.;
*   *power*—a shift in power within the organization, especially at the top, can cause dramatic change, particularly when responding to a crisis;
*   *competition*—a competitor's change in strategy might force our organization to change its strategy;

Who is driving the change? Change is usually initiated by an organization's executives, or by specialists or consultants called in as advisors.

Our willingness to support change is influenced by how legitimate we feel the initiator's motives are. If we believe the motives are self-serving, instead of doing what's best for the company, we'll be more likely to resist the change than support it. Trust plays a major role in our attitude toward change, particularly in whether or not there seem to be good reasons for the change. As a matter of fact, consultants or outside experts are often brought in to make decisions appear more legitimate.

What must be changed? We need to be sure that everyone understand what needs to change, in terms of people, structure, technology, and processes.

People changes may include changing the culture, or part of it, or introducing new skills, capabilities, or expertise that will be important in the future.

Structural changes are often the most far-reaching, because can they involve changes in authority, responsibilities, reward systems, procedures, or resource allocation.

Technological changes may include new equipment, new expertise, or changes in job responsibilities and assignments.

Process changes are most likely to affect communication patterns, coordination of activities, or decision- making.

How the change will be accomplished will be foremost in everyone's mind. A good way to encourage *support* rather than resistance, is ask the people who will be affected most by the change to help determine *how* it should be done.

When the change will need to take place will be determined by two factors: 1) when does it *need* to to be done? (i.e., what's the a deadline?); and 2) *how* it will be done (i.e., *what* are the things that need to be done, and in what order?) The details of the plan for change should be outlined as far in advance as possible, and shared with those who will be involved and those who will be affected.

One of the major reasons so many organizations resist change is that most of them, particularly the larger ones, are designed for efficiency. The quest for efficiency usually involves standardizing activities to make them more routine, formal documentation of policies and procedures, top-down decision-making, and reward systems that discourage risk-taking.

All of that is done in the interest of maintaining control; a fundamental goal of any bureaucracy. Since they depend on "sameness" for their consistency, these organizations discourage changing anything, or doing anything differently. And their managers avoid change for fear it will disrupt the status quo, or interfere with their ability to control the situation. But every organization has to change, sooner or later; if they don't they may not survive.

Change can be implemented either incrementally, or radically.

Incremental change is gradual. It requires seeing the need for change far enough in advance that there will be time to do it in small steps, made one at a time, *before* the change is necessary. Incremental change allows employees to change gradually, rather than all at once, a process that's much less threatening to them.

Radical change, on the other hand, is change that happens all at once; change that becomes necessary because an organization has resisted changing until it was in crisis, then was forced to change immediately, in order to survive. Unfortunately, the more bureaucratic the organization the more likely it will be to delay change until it is unavoidable, then have to do it radically.

Whether we make change incrementally or radically, the important thing is that we *choose* to do it, rather than waiting until we're *forced* to change. The key to making it a choice is to anticipate the need for change, by seeing it coming well in advance.

Sometimes change is for positive reasons, as when it's driven by the success of the organization. Changes brought about by organizational growth, for example, create "nice" problems, because growth is a good thing.

But employees find it much harder to accept changes that are necessary for survival, because they're usually caused by failures of the organization's management. It might be a failure to anticipate a decrease in sales, or a decision to outsource jobs to another organization, location, or country. Whatever the reason, it will harm employees' morale and loyalty to the company. That's why managing the change that comes from organizational decline is much more difficult than change that's brought about by growth, particularly when the decline leads to the need for downsizing.

DOWNSIZING

Because downsizing is one of the most traumatic and demoralizing actions any organization can undertake, it should only be done as a last resort, when there are no other options. But if it can't be avoided, how it's done will be critically important, because it will lay a foundation for future trust, or mistrust, between the organization's leaders and employees.

We won't attempt to cover the many detail of downsizing, but two issue are much too critical to ignore: who should be retained, and who should go; and how to treat those who lose their jobs.

The easiest way to downsize may appear to be to cut the same percentage of jobs—10 percent, for example—from every department. And, in fact, that's how it's done most often. While that may be easiest, and seen by many as fairest, it is seldom the best for the company. What's best for the company is doing it in a way that preserves the jobs that are most essential to the future.

With that in mind, the best way to downsize is to eliminate jobs based on their importance to the organization's strategy for the future. Every job should be listed, in the order of its *future* importance to the organization. Then, starting from the bottom of the list, those jobs that are *least* important should be eliminated first. That way the company keep the jobs, and people, who will be most difficult to replace, and on which the company's future will be built.

Every downsizing affects two groups of people: those who lose their jobs, and those who don't—the survivors. The way an organization treats the people who lose their jobs will also affect the survivors, and will be a major determinant of whether the long-term effects of the process will be positive or negative.

Those who survive a downsizing are likely to feel guilty, because they still have jobs while some of their friends have lost theirs. Organizational managers can either add to that guilt or ease it. If surviving employees see their departing friends being well treated, including assistance in finding new employment, it will not only help them feel less guilty, but will also reassure them that, if the same thing happens to them, they, too, will be treated fairly.

Another important step in rebuilding trust is to make sure the downsizing is done *all at one time*, rather than in stages. Any cutback should be large enough that the survivors can be assured that this will be the *only* layoff; there will be no more. Because if there has to be a second round, survivors will never again feel any job security. They will always be waiting for the next layoff, and the next.

FUTURE CHALLENGES/OPPORTUNITIES

Anticipating the need for change well in advance requires an organization to see major trends as they develop. Only then will they be able to visualize how those trends might affect the organization, and prepare for them well before the organization is affected.

Most major trends are visible long before they begin to affect us—often years in advance—which gives us plenty of time to prepare for them, *if* we see them coming. Seeing trends as they develop isn't difficult, if you're *looking* for them, which means, of course, you should *always* be scanning the horizon, looking for trends.

Following are examples of trends, in several major categories, that are currently visible:

Demographic/Social

- Labor force—growing
- Diversity (ethnic)—increasing—more minorities
- Age—aging population
    - longer life-spans
- Education levels—increasing
- Health—healthier life-styles
    - increasing obesity
- Geographic—population shifting:
    - to cities
    - to rural areas
    - to warmer climates
    - to beaches, mountains
- Immigration—increasing or decreasing?

Economic

- Consumers—increasing power
- Money—easier access to capital (for individuals)
- Incomes—disposable income increasing
- Interest rates—increasing or decreasing?

Globalization

- Economy—more worldwide, less national
- Labor market—more international, less national
- Competition—more worldwide, less national
- Population—worldwide changes and distributions
- Time and distance—compressed—world becoming flatter

Workplace

- Service jobs—increasing
- Manufacturing jobs—decreasing
- High-technology jobs—increasing
- Knowledge-based jobs—increasing
- Specialization—increasing (organizations, not workers)
- Productivity—increasing
- Younger workers (16-24)—increasing
- Older workers (55 and over)—increasing
- Contingency workers (temporary, part-time)—increasing
- Telecommuting—increasing
- Knowledge-based organizations:
  - more leadership, less management
  - more empowerment/participative management
  - increasing worker mobility = decreasing loyalty
  - quality of work-life becoming more important
- Employee rights—increasingly important
- Privacy—individual privacy, identity theft are concerns

- Attitudes toward work—balancing personal/family life with work life
- Culture—organizational cultures becoming more supportive
- Outsourcing—increasing or decreasing?

Government/Politics

- De-regulation—increasing or decreasing?
- Privatization—increasing or decreasing?
- Organizational boundaries (private, public, not-for-profit)—blurring
- Litigation—increasing
- Legislation (laws, regulations)—increasingly complex

Technology

- Wireless communication—increasing
- Internet use—increasing exponentially
- Biotechnology—emerging
- Nanotechnology (miniaturization)—emerging
- Information availability—increasing dramatically
- Telecommunications—global
- Mass customization = decreasing economies of scale

Education

- Education—becoming life-long learning
- Training—need is increasing
- Career development—essential for knowledge workers
- Learning organizations—increasing

Healthcare

- Costs—rising
- Preventive medicine—increasing

- Nurses—shortages, and increasing
- Doctors—shortages anticipated

The Physical Environment

- Environmental activism—increasing
- Environmental changes—perception vs. reality

SUMMARY

The world in which we live and work is constantly changing, and the way we respond to those changes can have a major influence on our success, as individuals and organizations. We should realize that change is always coming, but we don't always know what the change will be, or when, or where, or how.

But by watching trends, we can see things happening that are likely to affect us in the future. Trends in areas like demographics, the economy (national and global), legislation, and technology are not difficult to see, and we can often see them long before they start to affect us. Being aware of those trends will allow us, and our organizations, to make incremental changes well in advance, so we can reduce the probability of suddenly being faced with a crisis.

And leadership is the key; visionary leaders can help us see into the future, and lead us confidently forward, creating the kind of change, and the kind of future, that will inspire our optimism and enthusiasm.

REFERENCES

Amabile, T.M., Kramer, S.J., 2010, "What Really Motivates Workers: Understanding the Power of Progress." *Harvard Business Review*, Cambridge, MA: Harvard Business School Press, January-February: 43-46.

Barnard, C.I., 1938, *The Functions of the Executive*, Cambridge, MA: Harvard University Press

Bower, M., 1966, *The Will to Manage*, New York, NY: McGraw-Hill

Collins, J.C., 2001, *Good to Great*, New York, NY: HarperBusiness

Colvin, G., 1997, "The Changing Art of Becoming Unbeatable." *Fortune*, New York, NY: Time, Inc.

Craig, E., Kimberly, J.R., Cheese, P., 2009, "How to Keep Your Best Executives." *The Wall Street Journal*, October 26: R8

Fayol, H., 1916, *Administration Industrielle et Generale*, Paris: Dunod

Fisher, A., 2008, "Need to Know: E-mail is for Liars," *Fortune*, Nov. 24: 57

Griffin, R.W., 2008, *Fundamentals of Management*, New York: Houghton Mifflin

Katz, D., Kahn, R.L., 1966, *The Social Society of Organizations,* New York: John Wiley

Kouzes, J.M., Posner, B.Z., 2007, *The Leadership Challenge,* San Francisco: Jossey-Bass

March, J. G., Simon, H., 1958, *Organizations,* New York: John Wiley

Maslow, A.H., 1998, *Maslow on Management,* New York, NY: John Wiley & Sons

Mayo, E., 1933, *The Human Problems of Industrial Civilization,* New York: Macmillan

McGregor, D., 1960, *The Human Side of Enterprise,* New York, NY: McGraw-Hill

O'Neal, D., 2008, *Managing Strategically for Superior Performance,* Boston, MA: American Press

O'Neal, D., 2009, *Developing Leaders,* Boston, MA: American Press

Pfeffer, J., 1978, *Organizational Design,* Arlington Heights, IL: AHM Publishing

Scholtes, P.R., 1998, *The Leader's Handbook,* New York: McGraw-Hill

Sherman, A.W., Bohlander, G.W., Snell, S., 1996, *Managing Human Resources,* Cincinnati, OH: South-Western College Publishing

Simon, H.A., 1947, *Administrative Behavior: A Study of Decision-Making Processes in Administrative Organizations,* New York: Macmillan

Taylor, F.W., 1911, *The Principles of Scientific Management*, New York: Harper & Row

Weber, M., 1947, *The Theory of Social and Economic Organizations*, ed., Talcott Parsons, trans. A.M. Henderson and Talcott Parsons, New York: Free Press

Wellner, A.S., 2005, "Lost in Translation," *Inc.*, September:37-38